DINNING AS A ROMAN EMPERO

How to Cook Ancient Roman Recipes Today

Eugenia Salza Prina Ricotti

DINING AS A ROMAN EMPEROR

How to Cook Ancient Roman Recipes Today

«L'ERMA» di BRETSCHNEIDER

Eugenia Salza Prina Ricotti

DINING AS A ROMAN EMPEROR
How to Cook Ancient Roman Recipes Today

© Copyright 1993 «L'ERMA» di BRETSCHNEIDER
Via Cassiodoro, 19 - 00193 Roma - Italy
www.lerma.it

Reprinted 2010

Graphic layout by
«L'ERMA» di BRETSCHNEDER

Salza Prina Ricotti, Eugenia

Dining as a Roman emperor : how to cook ancient Roman recipes today / Eugenia Salza Prina Ricotti. - Roma : «L'ERMA» di BRETSCHNEIDER, 2010. - 116 p. : ill. ; 15x21 cm

ISBN 978-88-8265-589-1

CDD 21. 641.5937

1.   Culinaria - Roma antica
2.   Culinaria - Pompei - Antichità

INDEX

INTRODUCTION VII

GLOSSARY XI

APPETIZERS AND EGGS 1

SOUPS 15

MEAT 25

FISH 41
  The ancient recipes of Magna Graecia 43
  The recipes of the late Roman Empire 55

VEGETABLES 65

SWEETS, DESSERTS AND CHEESES 79

INTRODUCTION

A book about a famous ancient city, whether it be Babylon, Athens, Persepolis, Alexandria or, as in this case, Pompeii, is always like a voyage into a new world. Of all the cities that have emerged from the excavations of the past, Pompeii shows us its life most clearly. The others died slowly, and enough time has passed for them to have been stripped not only of their most important works of art and precious objects but of all those humble things that tell the stories of real human beings. For Pompeii, however, not only was death instantaneous but that last minute remained frozen by the blanket of lapilli that buried it — even if "frozen" seems an inappropriate term to describe a sea of fire and flames. Pompeii thus became our most precious source of information on the daily life of two thousand years

ago, and through it we know that part of its civilization that is nearest to us: the house as a place where people lived. Homes of every size and for every class of people, modest dwellings and luxurious residences in which it is possible to recreate the life lived there. Thus, with the help of the finds plus the information we can glean in the ancient authors, we can also reconstruct the history of ancient food, complete with recipes.

We might think that the daily meal is not a very important aspect of a civilization, but that would not be accurate. A people's diet and cuisine are an integral part of its individuality. After all, when we take a trip in a foreign country we do not usually limit ourselves to visiting monuments and museums, or buying so-called souvenirs from tacky shops; we also

try to find a characteristic place to eat where we can try some of the most typical dishes of the local cuisine. We may or may not like what we taste, but if the gastronomic experience was less than pleasant, satisfying our curiosity was important too.

Without a doubt many people feel this same curiosity, tempered by a certain diffidence, when it comes to ancient dishes. That diffidence derives from a number of strange and unfounded rumors regarding the ingredients of Roman dishes, propagated, printed and taught in schools by persons who, though undoubtedly well educated, nevertheless prove themselves to be less than seriously committed to the subject. To be perfectly blunt, they do not know what they are talking about. They have spread the notion that the Romans ate highly disgusting, even rotten, things. It is impossible to understand how they can have blithely accepted the idea that people so wealthy and so powerful could poison themselves at table, and stands — rather than sits — behind a counter, but the bread is always golden brown and fragrant, and there will always be a little boy tormenting his parents until they give in and buy him some cookies.

We see evidence of food and drink everywhere in Pompeii. The ubiquitous bars in Italian cities today can trace their ancestry to Roman times. When one was tired in the street and needed to quench one's thirst, there was always a *thermopolium* with its marble counter and enormous wine-filled *dolia* buried in the masonry. One could choose not only the type of wine and the amount of water to be added — because ʸin antiquity wine was always drunk diluted — but also whether to drink it piping hot or ice cold. In the shop, next to the counter, there was always a little hearth with the kettle of boiling water and, in summer, the better *thermopolia* were also equipped with snow. This costly commodity was collected dur-

ing winter on the highest mountain peaks, brought downhill wrapped in straw and woolen cloths and kept all summer in special storage places.

The finds from Pompeii constitute a vast documentation of the equipment used to handle food. Many of the objects can be seen in the Pompeii Antiquarium or in the National Museum in Naples. Pots of every shape, frying pans, grills, large and artistic bronze "samovars" for the triclinium to hold the boiling water needed to make the winter punch; meat hooks; measures for grains and all the utensils needed in the kitchen or for the serving of foods and for dining room use. Next to these, in the display cases we also find loaves of bread that were bought to eat that final day. Lentils, chickpeas, hazelnuts, walnuts, olives and more — all black and wizened now but once so good, waiting to go into the dinner that was never cooked.

Let us take a look at this dinner. Our point of departure is the recipes found in the ancient texts. As far as Roman cooking is concerned, these begin with the recipes that Cato the Censor (234-149 B.C.) included in

his treatise on agriculture. He did it for an excellent reason: in fact, if the poor man did not want to eat polenta of spelt every day of his life, he had to tell the farmwife how to vary the dinner a bit. There were, in fact, numerous cookbooks, especially in the Greek world. We know of some twenty-two; in many cases we just have a small excerpt, and of still others we know only the name of the author and the title, as, for example, that of a certain Mithaecus cited by Plato in the *Gorgias* as the author of a treatise on Sicilian cooking. There were fewer Latin ones, but in compensation the only cookbook to have survived in its entirety is the Latin *De re coquinaria* by a certain Apicius: not the famous patrician Apicius who lived in the reign of Tiberius, and certainly not a patrician. Very likely, the author was a professional cook who — to judge from his rather coarse and decadent Latin — must have lived around the fourth century A.D.

The *De re coquinaria* is not a great cookbook. It is a congeries of recipes drawn from here and there, including from the diets of medical books. Moreover, it was written for other cooks, who, we presume, were well able to gauge quantities, cooking times and temperatures. It is essentially a long list of ingredients, many of which force us today to consult botanical texts to find out what they are. Despite its short-comings, however, *De re coquinaria* is one of the main documents on ancient Roman cooking, and we are obliged to use it in order to reconstruct something of ancient Roman cooking. Since Pompeii was also influenced by contacts with many areas of the Mediterrane-an, neither can we neglect the information provided by other texts that talk about cooking, especially the Greek and Sicilian ones.

The ancient Roman dinner — What might dinner have been like in Pompeii under the Romans? There, as in the rest of the Empire, dinner was the main meal of the day. Life in those days was regulated by the sun. The Romans rose early and had a good breakfast of bread, meat and cheese. Often these were leftovers from the previous evening, which guests customarily took home wrapped in a napkin, called *mappa,* which they carried at all times. Around noon, they had a light snack and, after going to the baths, around three or four in the afternoon, began their dinner. Dinner guests would remove their shoes as soon as they arrived, and if need be, even wash their feet before taking their places on the couches of the *triclinium.* They reclined upon mattresses covered with linen sheets fresh from the laundry, resting their elbow on the cushions to begin the sumptuous meal.

GLOSSARY

Some notes on what the Roman ingredients are, including where to find them or what to substitute for them in the recipes.

ALICA. This was the product of one of the first cereals to be cultivated in antiquity, spelt (*Triticum dicoccum,* Schrk.). The grain is hard and very difficult to separate from the chaff. To do so, the Romans roasted the spelt and then pounded it for a long time in wooden mortars with pestles covered with sheets of iron. The job was so unpleasant that it was assigned as punishment to the slaves in chains who had been convicted of the worst misdeeds. From this they derived the *alica,* a highly prized type of semolina. There existed three distinct kinds of *alica,* distinguished by its size. The finest, and most costly, *alica* was rubbed white with a special clay, evidently sulfurous, taken from a hill called Leucogea (meaning "white ground" in Greek), located between Puteoli and Naples. The Romans used *alica* to make polentas (note that polenta is not necessarily made with corn, which the Romans, of course, did not have), creams and stuffings; but they also made *tractae* with it — thin sun-dried or baked wafers used in cooking. Hard-wheat semolina is the best modern substitute for *alica.*

BAY LEAVES (*Laurus nobilis*). The bay laurel is usually cultivated as a hedge or bush. The Romans used bay leaves to make triumphal wreaths, but in cooking actually preferred the berries to the leaves, though they used them too. Bay is often found in pork recipes.

BULBI (*Muscari comosum,* Mill.). These bulbs look like small red onions but have a very different taste. They are extremely difficult to find except in southern Italy, where they are called *lampacioni* (pronounced lampachoni). *Bulbi* are exceedingly bitter and must be boiled in several changes of salted water until they lose their bitter taste. In Puglia they are eaten preserved in vinegar and are still reputed to be an aphrodisiac.

CARAWAY (*Carum carvi, L.*). This is a biennial herb, an umbellifer that reaches heights of 2 feet. It is easy to grow and will seed itself if the seeds are not harvested. The wild grain is smaller than that of cumin, but it has a more pronounced flavor.

CAROENUM. Grape must, boiled until it is reduced to two thirds of its volume. It was used as a sweetener in place of the more expensive honey.

CATNIP (*Calamintha officinalis, L.*). A wild mint-like herb, much used by the Romans. Its name comes from the fact that cats are very attracted by it. They eat the leaves and roll about frenetically rubbing them-selves on the bushes.

CELERY (*Apium graveolens, L.*). There is not much to say about our old friend the celery except to observe that the Roman one was not the fleshy-stalked variety we find today. It was a much smaller, much greener plant. Some varieties are still grown simply as herbs in the vegetable gardens of the countryside. Celery seeds are sold in supermarket spice sections.

CHIVES (*Allium schoenoprasum, L.*). The thin, tubular leaves are used. Fresh chives are sold in bunches, but the plant is easy to grow in pots. Chives have a pleasant onion taste. The Romans used them raw, as we still do, to flavor cheeses, sauces and a wide variety of dishes.

CORIANDER LEAVES (*Coriandrum sativum, L.*). Both the green leaves (also known as cilantro or Chinese parsley) and the seeds of this plant can be used. Just remember that the leaves have a completely different flavor from the seeds. In Asia and Latin America it is sold in bunches like parsley, which, with its serrated leaves, it closely resembles, but only on the outside. The taste is another thing entirely. The name — from the Greek *koris,* which means "bedbug," — derives from the smell of the green leaves. This discouraging information is a warning that, even today, many people truly hate the taste of coriander leaves, and so this ingredient should usually be replaced with common parsley.

CORIANDER SEEDS (*Coriandrum sativum, L.*). These are ubiquitous on the spice shelves of super-markets.

CUMIN (*Cuminum sativum, L.*). This delicate annual herb grows in warm climates. It is cultivated especially in North Africa, Sicily, the Middle East, India and the Americas. In Europe it tends to be confused with caraway, because the seeds are quite similar in appearance, although their fragrance is different. Cumin seeds can be bought either ground or whole.

DEFRUTUM. Grape must boiled until it is reduced to one half or one third its volume. It was used as a sweetener in place of honey, which was much more expensive.

DILL (*Anethum graveolens, L.*). This is an annual or biennial plant with filiform (thread-like) leaves and small yellow flowers; it grows 2-3 feet tall. It was appreciated by both the Greeks and the Romans. Dill can be bought fresh and dried (though there is no comparison). It is advisable to grow it at home in the garden or in pots.

FETA. A white cheese widely used in Greece, Bulgaria and Turkey. It is soaked in water and is usually very salty. It is found in the better food stores of large cities.

GARUM. This is one of the most misunderstood and maligned of ancient ingredients. The origin of the problem is a remark of Pliny the Elder that *garum* was "the liquid of rotten fish," a definition that for centuries has weighed like a millstone on the gastronomy of the ancient Romans. Fortunately, recipes for making *garum* have come down to us, so we can easily see that the method was the same as the standard Italian method still in use for preserving anchovies in salt. In fact, the equivalent of *garum is* employed with excellent results in the cuisines of a number of Asian countries. As for *liquamen* (see below), the best substitute nowadays is an Asian product called nuoc-nam. In some cases, however, it is better to stick with plain salt. Of course, not even nuoc-nam is easy to find, so one can manage by salting the food a little less and adding a bit of anchovy dissolved in oil. (Put a little olive oil in a pan and heat the anchovy slowly, mashing it with a fork until it is completely disintegrated.)

LASER or SILPHIUM. Another lost ingredient. The most celebrated and sought after silphium in antiquity, from the Cyrenaica, in present-day eastern Libya, was a wild plant that grew in the North African desert fringe but had become extinct as early as the reign of Nero. The last, precious specimen was found and sent to the emperor as a gift. Since silphium could not be cultivated, it all ended there. People began to use a similar plant, asafetida, which grew in Afghanistan and Pakistan and whose product is still widely used in Far Eastern cooking. In small doses, it imparts a pleasant garlicky taste to food, but use just a bit too much (it takes almost nothing) and the food will taste so horrible that the whole dish has to be thrown away. This is why garlic is always used instead.

LIGUSTICUM (*Levisticum officinale*). The Latin means lovage or love parsley, and it is found in nearly all the recipes in *De re coquinaria*. It is no longer cultivated today, and we do not know why. However, it is not extinct. Botanical gardens and greenhouses sell the seeds, and it can be grown in a pot. Its pleasant flavor is a cross between celery and parsley, which have replaced it, and the substitute is a mixture of celery and parsley.

LIQUAMEN. This Latin word is used for a brine that can be flavored with a wide variety of sub-stances. Thus at times *garum is* called *liquamen*, fish brine, and Varro provides the recipe for *a liquamen* of pears. When an ancient recipe calls for *liquamen* we can safely replace it with salt without greatly altering the flavor, although purists will want to use nuoc-nam (see below), available in specialty food shops.

MARJORAM (*Origanum majorana* or *Majorana hortensis, L.*). A plant of the family of oregano, but the scent is similar to that of thyme, which it often replaces. It can be easily grown in pots, and is sold dried in all food stores.

MINT. Of the many kinds of mint, two are found most often in ancient Roman recipes.

Pennyroyal (*Mentha pulegium, L.*). Called *puleium* in Latin, this is the wild mint that is found in meadows and that was much used in ancient Roman peasant dishes. Today it is known in Rome as *mentuccia* (pronounced mentu-cha) and is an essential flavoring in *carciofi* (pronounced carchofi, artichokes) *alla romana.*

Garden mint (Mentha spicata). The oldest variety of mint and probably the one intended in the ancient recipes. The Romans spread it throughout Europe as far as Britain. It is the character-istic flavoring of the peasant dish-es of ancient Rome, which were never without it. It can be bought anywhere.

MYRTLE (*Myrtis communis*). A typical Mediterranean plant, myrtle is an evergreen bush with straight branches and small, fragrant leaves. Until the second century A.D. the Romans, who did not yet have pep-per (which was later imported from India), used dried myrtle berries in its stead, which, of course, did not re-semble pepper in the slightest. Myr-tle berries have a pleasant scent and

should be picked and experimented with in the kitchen. On the rocky hills of Italy's seacoast, there is al-ways an abundance of myrtle, and in the late summer one can gather in a good supply.

NUOC-NAM. This is a brine much used in the cooking of Indochina and, like *garum,* is the liquid thrown off during the salting process of dif-ferent kinds of fish. The procedure is identical to that used in the classi-cal period for the much-maligned Roman condiment. Nuoc-nam is ex-cellent for cooked foods, but it is not advisable for raw. In fact, in Roman times not all *garum* was suitable for dressing salads, for which they prob-ably used the type that, in the words of Pliny the Elder, "has the color of honey and is so good that you can drink it."

OREGANO (*Origanum vulgare, L.*). Oregano is very well known, and almost everyone likes it. It grows spontaneously on rocky, sunny hills, and is common in the entire Medi-terranean basin, where its powerful scent is a feature of summer walks

on sun-drenched rocky coasts. Al-though it's usually found in jars, some-times you can buy the little branches tied in bunches from herb-alists. When you need some, you rub a branch between the hands, letting the fragrant tiny leaves fall into the sauce.

PASSOLONE. This is an Italian word, a type of typically Sicilian seasoned olive. When the olives are very ripe they fall to the ground. They are then picked up and treated with salt and seasoned with wild fennel seeds. They can then be eaten plain or used in cooking. Despite their wrinkled appearance, they are still very fleshy. They are hard to find outside Sicily, and the easier to find and very similar Tunisian ones can substitute.

PINE NUTS. This well-known ingre-dient was much used in ancient Ro-man cooking. They can be bought in grocery stores or from herbalists.

RUE (*Ruta graveolens, L.*). This large (up to 3 feet in height), strong-smelling bush has small bluish leaves and yellow flowers. Not everyone likes its strong scent and bitter flavor, but the Romans used it widely and introduced it into many conquered countries, including Britain. Only the leaves are used. It must be bought from herbalists.

SAVORY (*Satureja hortensis, L.*). A low (12 inches) annual plant, it is slender and erect with thin stems and narrow leaves about three-fourths of an inch long. Its fragrance is similar to that of thyme but is more bitter, much more penetrating, and, used to excess, can ruin a dish. It must be home grown, and green-houses sell both the seeds and the plant in pots.

SESAME (*Sesamum indicum, L.*). This tropical herb came originally from India. The Romans used sesame seeds to flavor cheese and liked their walnut-like flavor. The scent is heightened if the seeds are toasted lightly before use. Sesame is easy to find in ordinary grocery stores.

THYME. There are several varieties, all with a very strong fragrance. The main ones and those used by the Romans are:

Thyme (*Thymus vulgaris, L.*). A small, bushy perennial plant with a woody trunk, small gray-green leaves and purple flowers. It grows well in pots, but should be transplanted every once in a while. The wild variety, found in Mediterranean countries, has a very penetrating fragrance and is without doubt superior to the cultivated kind. It is known from earliest antiquity; the name is Greek, but the Romans much appreciated it. It is very easy to find.

Bronze Kitchen ware

Wild thyme or continental thyme (*Thymus serpyllum, L.*). This plant crawls on the ground. When planted in a sunny dry location, it forms a thick, compact carpet and so is often used in forms of gardening as, for example, rock gardens. Its fragrance is strong and very pleasant.

WILD FENNEL (*Foeniculum vulgare*, var. *dulce, sativum*, etc.). Found in Mediterranean meadows in springtime, this is a plant of the family Umbelliferae. Both its filiform leaves and highly fragrant seeds are used. The young leaves are eaten in various ways. The seeds are used to flavor pork, salamis (like the famous Tuscan *finocchiona*), and certain delicious Sicilian sausages. It occurs in ancient Roman recipes in both leaf and seed form. The green tops of ordinary fennel can substitute if need be.

OTHERS. Obviously the recipes call for still other ingredients that are difficult to find today. These will be noted as they come up, along with remote possibilities of substitution. The glossary contains only the basic ones. Now let's cook.

Terms explained in the glossary are marked with an asterisk (*).

Glassware and pottery

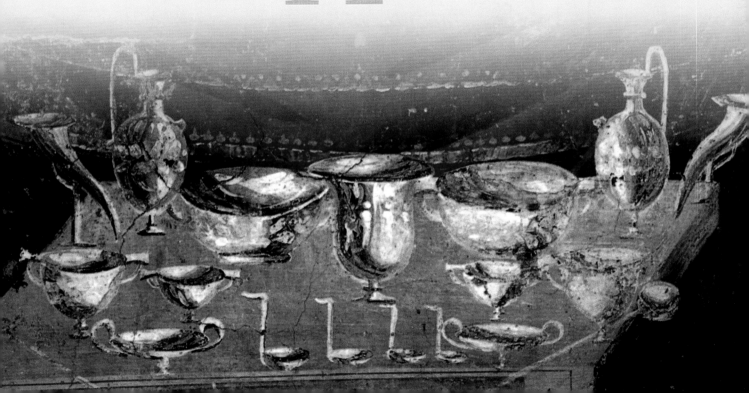

Appetizer and eggs

The Herculaneum Gate seen from outside

CATO'S *LIBUM*

EXCELLENT WITH COCKTAILS

Make libum *like this. Pound well in a mortar two pounds of cheese. When it is thoroughly macerated, add a pound of wheat flour and knead well with the cheese or, if you want a more delicate cake, use half a pound of fine flour. Add an egg and knead again carefully. Form a loaf, put it on a bed of leaves and bake it slowly on a warm hearth under a clay pot.*

CATO, *De agricultura* LXXV

LIBUM (serves 6)

Ricotta or any fresh cheese	14 oz
Flour	3.5 oz
Egg	1
Salt	pinch

Cato's recipe is for one loaf, but today it is much more practical to divide the dough into small pieces shaped like rolls, which, can be served as a bread, and, piping hot, with aperitifs. It is best to make them about 2 inches in diameter. They will expand in the oven, so remember to leave some space between them. The dough comes out very soft and tends to stick to the hands when you form the rolls. The work is easier if for each one you roll a scant tablespoon of dough in a little flour, then form a ball and flatten it. Then put it over an oiled bay leaf on an oiled oven tile. When all the dough it used up, put the rolls in the oven at 350°F (180°C) for 25 minutes. *Libum* is excellent with cocktails for a party or buffet dinner. You can double or triple the quantities, depending on the number of guests, but remember to use only one egg for up to 1 lb 12 oz of ricotta.

The ricotta or fresh cheese used in this recipe should be unpasteurized, and the success of the recipe cannot be guaranteed with pasteurized ones.

SCRIBLITA

LIKE TURKISH BOUREK, IT CAN BE SERVED WITH APERITIFS

Make scriblita *like this. Make the crust, the* tracta *and the filling exactly as for* placenta *but omit the honey.*

CATO, *De agricultura* LXXVIII

SCRIBLITA (serves 6)

Flour	9 oz
Water	as needed
Salt	pinch
Semolina	9 oz
Ricotta or (even better) feta*	1.1 lb
Salt	to taste

Make a thin pastry dough with the flour and water. Dissolve the ricotta or feta. Add some salt if you use ricotta, but never salt feta, which is quite salty on its own. If you are determined, make the *tractae* by kneading water and semolina, then divide the dough into 5 equal parts, roll them with a rolling pin to a thickness of 1/8 inch, and set them aside. When they are quite dry, rub them with oil and put them in the oven until they are crisp and golden. You can, however, skip this whole, long operation and use matzos. Cover an oven tile with oiled bay leaves, spread over these the sheet of dough made with flour and water, letting it hang down, and then put one of the matzos on top, in the middle. Cover it with a layer of cheese and continue alternating matzo and filling until all the ingredients are used up. Pull up the outer sheet and seal it in the middle. Oil the whole thing and, if desired, brush the surface with beaten egg. Put it in an oven preheated to 320°F (160°C) until the crust is cooked through and golden brown.

3 *E*PITYRUM

KEEP IT ON HAND FOR HORS D'OEUVRES, COCKTAILS AND COMPANY

Recipe for a relish of green, ripe and black olives. Remove the pit from green, ripe and black olives, and proceed as follows: chop the flesh and add oil, vinegar, coriander, cumin, fennel, rue and mint. Put them in an earthenware dish, cover them with oil and serve.

CATO, *De agricultura* CXIX

OLIVE CAVIAR

Pitted black olives	11 oz
Coriander seeds*	pinch
Cumin*	pinch
Wild fennel*	pinch
Rue*	tiny amount
Mint*	pinch Olive oil (extra virgin if possible) as needed
Vinegar	as needed

Take a glass jar of the desired size and as large a quantity of olives as will fill it after they have been pitted and chopped (their volume will be greatly reduced). The olives that give the best results are those called "passolone" in Sicily or else Tunisian ones. Combine the herbs and the pitted olives in a blender and process well at the minimum speed. Then, little by little add oil and vinegar, raise the speed to the maximum and process for at least 1 minute. Rue goes very well with this combination of flavors but only in minuscule quantities. Do not worry if you cannot find rue: the final product will not be very different. When every-thing is well reduced and looks almost like caviar, check the seasoning, and if needed, add a little salt, more oil or more vinegar. Put the epityrum in the jar, cover with a layer of oil, and store in the refrigerator.

4 BLACK OLIVES

KEEP ON HAND FOR HORS D'OEUVRES, COCKTAILS AND COMPANY

Afterwards comes the cold winter during which the olive harvest again requires the attention of the farm-wife... [it is at this moment that] *the olives of Pausias, the* orchitae [large highly prized olives] *and even those of Nevi are prepared to serve them at dinners for company. ... These olives are put in a jar and the jar is filled completely with* sapa *or with* defrutum, *covering the olives with a small bunch of wild fennel pushed well down to hold it. Many people prefer to mix three parts of boiled grape must* [some prefer two] *with one of vinegar and they keep the olives in this marinade.*

COLUMELLA, *De re rustica* XII.L

OLIVES FOR ANTIPASTO

Put Gaeta-type or Greek olives in a jar and make a marinade that will fill the jar. Maintain the following proportions:

*Defrutum** or honey	3 parts
Vinegar	1 part
Wild fennel*	1 small bunch

Push the olives down toward the bottom of the jar, and pour the marinade over them, keeping them down with a dried sprig of wild fennel stuck into the jar in such a way that the olives remain submerged and do not stick up. The fennel will give the olives a very pleasant fragrance. They will be ready to eat in about two weeks.

SALA CATTABIA

THE ANCESTOR OF THE ITALIAN *PANZANELLA* — PERFECT FOR A SUMMER DINNER

Pepper, mint, celery, dried pennyroyal, cheese, pine nuts, honey, vinegar, brine, egg yolks, cool water. Take bread first dunked in water and vinegar and then squeezed out, cow's-milk cheese, cucumbers, and put them in a small bowl, breaking up the pine nuts. Add capers, chopped finely, and chicken livers. Pour over the sauce and put the container over ice-cold water and serve.

APICIUS, *De re coquinaria* IV.I.1

SALA CATTABIA-1 (serves 6)

Good quality bread	10 1/2 oz	Honey	2 tablespoons
Gruyere cheese	2 oz	Vinegar	2 tablespoons
Cucumber	1	Egg	1 yolk
Chicken livers	3	Anchovies packed in salt	3
Pine nuts	1 handful	Ice water	a little
Pepper	to taste	Salt	to taste
Pennyroyal*	1 bunch		
Celery	1 rib		

Dip the bread in water and vinegar and then squeeze. In a small bowl layer the moistened bread, the cucumber, sliced thin, the capers, the chicken livers cooked in a little wine, and the pine nuts. Process the remaining ingredients in a blender to make a sauce and pour into the bowl on top of the bread and cucumber mixture. Chill well in the refrigerator, then serve.

SALA CATTABIA

FRESH AND TASTY FOR A SUMMER DINNER

Take a loaf of Alexandrian bread without the crust, dunk it in water and vinegar. Put in a mortar pepper, honey, mint, garlic, coriander leaves, salted cow's-milk cheese, water and oil. Place the container over snow and serve.

APICIUS, *De re coquinaria* IV.I.2

SALA CATTABIA-2 (serves 6)

Pepper	generous amount
Honey	3 teaspoons
Roman mint	1/2 handful
Garlic	2 cloves
Green coriander*	1/2 handful
Parmesan cheese	2 oz
Olive oil	3 tablespoons
Water	as needed
Soft bread crumbs	10 1/2 oz

Soak the bread crumbs in water and squeeze, then put them in a small bowl. Process all the other ingredients in a blender. If you do not have coriander leaves, use parsley. Pour this sauce over the bread, put the bowl in the refrigerator and chill well before serving.

OVA FRIXA

DELECTABE!

Oenogarata.

Apicius, VII.XIX.1

OENOGARATA SAUCE FOR FRIED EGGS (serves 6)

Eggs	12
Pepper	1 level teaspoon
Nuoc-nam*	4 tablespoons
Dry wine	4 tablespoons
Sweet wine	4 tablespoons
Olive oil	8 tablespoons

Make the sauce: crush the pepper and moisten it with the nuoc-nam. (More simply, instead of nuoc-nam, use 3 or 4 anchovy fillets, dissolved in a little olive oil over low heat, and salt to taste) Then add the dry wine, the sweet wine and the olive oil. Put the mixture in a small saucepan and bring to the boil, then pour it into a sauce boat. Fry the eggs and serve the sauce on the side.

OVA ELIXA

A VARIATION SPECIAL ENOUGH FOR EASTER LUNCH

Liquamen, *oil, pure wine or* liquamen, *pepper and* laser.

APICIUS, VII.XIX.2

SAUCE FOR HARD-COOKED EGGS (serves 6)

Eggs	12
Nuoc-nam*	4 tablespoons
Strong wine	5 teaspoons
Olive oil	8 teaspoons
or	
Pepper	1 teaspoon
Nuoc-nam*	4 tablespoons
Laser or garlic	trace

Hard-cook the eggs, and serve with either of two sauces: either nuoc-nam, pure wine and olive oil, or nuocnam, pepper and *laser*. More simply, instead of nuoc-nam, use 3 or 4 anchovy fillets dissolved in olive oil (better actually), and instead of hard-to-find *laser*, use the juice of a small garlic clove. Both these sauces should be boiled and served in sauce boats with the eggs.

In ovis apalis

VERY GOOD, ESPECIALLY IF YOU USE ANCHOVIES

Pepper, ligusticum, *softened pine nuts. Moisten with honey, vinegar and dilute with* liquamen.

APICIUS, VII.XIX.3

SAUCE FOR BOILED EGGS

Pepper	1/4 oz
Ligusticum*	1 handful of leaves
Pine nuts	1 oz
Honey	2 teaspoons
Vinegar	3 tablespoons
Nuoc-nam*	3 tablespoons or anchovy fillets dissolved in olive oil

Process all the ingredients together in a blender. Serve in a sauce boat with eggs boiled until the whites are firm but the yolks are still runny (5 minutes). If you don't have *ligusticum,* you can substitute an equal amount of half celery and half parsley, and, if you don't have the nuoc-nam either, use anchovies dissolved over low heat and salt to taste.

PATINA URTICARUM

EXCELLENT FOR A LIGHT SPRING SUPPER

Take some nettles, wash them, drain them, dry them on a board and then cut them in small pieces. Chop 10 scruples of pepper, moisten with liqua-men, and rub the mixture hard against the sides of a mortar. Then add 2 cyathi of liquamen, 6 ounces of oil. Boil in a pot. When it has boiled, put it to cool. Then oil a baking pan and break into it 8 eggs and beat them. [Add the nettles to the eggs] in the baking pan and place in hot cinders so it is covered below and on top of [the lid].

APICIUS, IV.II.36

NETTLE PIE (serves 6)

Pepper	1/4 oz
Nuoc-nam*	8 tablespoons
Olive oil	9 tablespoons
Eggs	8
Nettles	2 lb 3 oz

The recipe can be used for other greens as well, even ones the Romans did not have, such as spinach. But it is best made in spring with nettles. Put on a pair of thick gardening gloves and gather the tender tips of the nettles. Wash them, drain them, and dry them well, and then chop them. Crush the pepper in a mortar and moisten it with a tablespoon of nuoc-nam. Put everything in a sauce-pan with the oil and the rest of the nuoc-nam and boil. (Remember that instead of nuoc-nam you can per-fectly well use 3 or 4 anchovy fillets dissolved in oil.) Cool the nettle mix-ture, then add the 8 eggs, beaten as for an omelet. Oil a pan and, if you have a fireplace or barbecue, put it over the coals, covering the lid with coals as well. Preheat the oven to 265°F (130°C). Set the pan in anoth-er pan partially filled with water and bake for 1 hour 15 minutes. Remove the pan from the oven and sprinkle the pie with pepper. It can be eaten hot or cold.

TYROTARICHUM
ONE OF CICERO'S FAVORITE DISHES

Cook salted fish in oil and then bone it. Take cooked brains, the pieces of fish, chicken giblets, 2 hard-cooked eggs, fresh cheese, parboiled, and put everything together to heat in a skillet. Chop pepper, levisticum, oregano, rue berries, wine, sweet wine, oil and put everything in a skillet over the flame to cook them. At the end, bind everything with raw egg. Put on a platter, sprinkle with chopped cumin and serve.

APICIUS, *De re coquinaria* IV.II.17

TYROTARICHUM, FISH AND CHEESE PIE (serves 6-8)

Tuna packed in oil	7 oz can	*Ligusticum**	2 handfuls
Oregano	1 generous pinch	Hard-cooked eggs, quartered	2
Lamb or calf brains	7 oz	Rue	2 berries
Various leftovers	7 oz	Dry white wine	8 tablespoons
Fresh cheese	7 oz	Marsala	4 tablespoons
Olive oil	4 tablespoons	Eggs (raw)	10
Pepper	1 pinch		

Combine in a bowl the tuna, the quartered hard-cooked eggs, the lamb or calf brains, parboiled, refreshed in cold water, peeled and trimmed, and the fresh cheese, diced, or feta (Greek, Bulgarian, or Turkish cheese) rinsed free of salt in water. You can also add pieces of leftover fish. Put the mixture in a skillet with a little oil and let the flavors blend over low heat. Meanwhile, chop together the pepper, the *ligusticum* (or equal parts of celery and parsley), the oregano and the rue berries. Dilute with the wine, the Marsala and the oil, then pour everything into the skillet over the other ingredients, and cook, stirring, over a low flame until almost all the liquid has evaporated. At this point, add the raw eggs, beaten well, and let them cook and brown on both sides, like a sort of omelet or pie. Put on a serving dish, sprinkle with the chopped cumin and serve.

F*LAN*

A DELICATE SUPPER DISH

Pine nuts, broken walnut kernels. Toast them and chop them. Mix them with honey, pepper, liquamen, *milk, eggs. A little oil.*

APICIUS, IV.II.2

WALNUT FLAN (serves 6)

Milk	3 cups
Eggs	8
Pine nuts	3 1/2 oz
Walnut meats	3 1/2 oz
Honey	1 tablespoon
Nuoc-nam*	3 tablespoons or
Salt	2 scant teaspoons
Pepper	generous amount

Toast the pine nuts and walnut meats lightly in a skillet with a tiny quantity of oil. You will need a ring mold, 12 inches in diameter and 4 inches deep. Put the milk in a bowl and add the honey and the nuoc-nam (in this flan the 2 teaspoons of salt actually work better). Beat the eggs as for an omelet, add them to the milk mixture and stir well, then strain through a sieve, add the pine nuts and the walnut meats, put the mixture into the mold. Set the mold in a larger, lower pan full of boiling water, bake in a low oven for 1 hour 15 minutes. Turn out the flan, sprinkle with plenty of pepper, and serve.

Soups

Ruins of the temple of Isis

13

AMULATUM ALITER

A LIGHT SOUP SUITABLE FOR CHILDREN OR DELICATE STOMACHS

Make a broth with chicken bones. Then throw into the pot leek, dill, salt. When it is done, add pepper, celery seeds, then reduce to a mush the rice, add liquamen, *and sweet wine or* defrutum, *mix everything and serve with meatballs.*

APICIUS, *De re coquinaria* II.II.9

CREAM OF RICE (serves 6)

Unsalted chicken broth	7 cups
Leeks	2
Dill	1 pinch
Cream of rice	6 tablespoons
Nuoc-nam*	6 tablespoons
Sweet wine	3 teaspoons

Put the broth, the leeks, finely sliced, and the dill into a saucepan. Just when it comes to the boil, add the cream of rice without stopping stirring, to prevent lumps from forming.

Flavor with *liquamen,* which serves as salt, but remember that it can be replaced with 1 tablespoon oil in which 2 anchovy fillets have been dissolved, or more simply just with salt.

If desired, add small meatballs (made with your favorite recipe), which will make this cream of rice a rich and nutritious dish. Taste and, if needed, add salt or nuoc-nam.

14 PATINA COTIDIANA (PASTA CASSEROLE)

A DELICIOUS AND ORIGINAL FIRST COURSE

Take cooked pieces of sow's udder, cooked fish, small pieces of cooked chicken. All these things cut them carefully. Take a bronze skillet and, after having broken some eggs into a bowl, beat them. Put in a mortar pepper, ligusticum, *rub them, moisten them with* liquamen, *wine and sweet wine and a little oil and boil in a small pot. when they have come to the boil, bind the sauce. Add the meat pieces to the sauce; put in the bottom of a bronze baking pan* a diploidem *(sheet of dough), pour over it oil and a ladleful of sauce, then* a laganum *[layer of lasagna] and continue like that. For each sheet of lasagna, add as many ladlefuls of sauce. At the last, put a sheet after piercing it with a straw.* [Cook.] *Unmold onto a platter and add pepper.*

APICIUS, *De re coquinaria* IV.II.15

BAKED LASAGNE (serves 6)

Pasta for lasagne	1 lb	Marsala	1/2 cup
Pepper	1 generous pinch	Nuoc-nam*	3 tablespoons
*Ligusticum**	1 handful	Broth	4 cups
Wine	1 cup	Egg yolks	3-4
Leftover meat, chicken, fish, ham, etc.		Starch	4 tablespoons

In a blender jar put the pepper, celery and parsley (if not using *ligusticum*), the wine and the Marsala, dilute with the broth, and season with nuoc-nam or with salt. Then, more or less as for paella, add whatever leftovers of meat, fish and cold cuts that you have on hand and add them to the sauce. Simmer slowly for about 2 hours until completely blended; at the end, bind the sauce with the egg yolks and the starch. Finally, put a bit of sauce in the bottom of a baking pan, and then place a sheet of pasta on top, and continue alternating layers, covering each sheet of pasta with ladlefuls of sauce. Prick small holes in the last sheet of pasta with a toothpick. Pour over a generous amount of sauce and place the pan either on a very large burner on top of the stove or in an oven preheated to 350°F (180°C). If you choose the oven, be sure to cover the pan with its lid and to place it in a larger pan of water so that the top layer of pasta does not get dry. Bake for 18 minutes. It should be noted that the Romans made their dough for lasagne only with hard-wheat flour and water, never with egg.

TISANE
EXCELLENT FOR FAMILY DINNERS OR IN THE COUNTRY

Soak chickpeas, lentils and dried peas. Rub barley to remove the chaff and boil it with the other legumes. When they are done, add oil and cut up leek, green coriander leaves, dill, and wild fennel and throw them in the pot. Boil cabbage tops and chop together a goodly quantity of wild fennel, oregano, silphium and fennel. When they are chopped, flavor with liquamen *and add them to the legumes. Finally, put very tender chopped cabbage leaves on top.*

APICIUS, *De re coquinaria* IV.IV.2

LEGUME SOUP (serves 6)

Water	6 cups	Vinegar	1 dash
Chickpeas	3 1/2 oz	Broccoli flowerets	7 oz
Dried peas	3 1/2 oz	Oregano	1 generous pinch
Lentils	3 1/2 oz	Garlic cloves	2
Pearl barley	3 1/2 oz	*Ligusticum**	1 handful
Nuoc-nam*	2 tablespoons	Olive oil	2 tablespoons
Parsley	1 handful		

Soak the chickpeas, peas, and barley overnight and then boil them in the 6 cups of cold salted water. Par-boil the broccoli in salted water. Put in the saucepan the leek, sliced thin, the wild fennel, the dill, the oregano, the *ligusticum* (or equal amounts celery and parsley), coarsely chopped. Add to the pot the nuocnam (or 2 anchovy fillets dissolved over heat in oil and a bit of salt dissolved in a little water). Taste, and add salt or nuoc-nam if needed. Before serving garnish with shredded tender cabbage leaves.

Julian polenta

EXCELLENT ONE-DISH MEAL FOR A WINTER EVENING

Soak carefully hulled alica and cook until it comes to a boil. When it boils, add oil and when it begins to thicken, stir carefully. Take two cooked brains and half a pound of meat ground as for meatballs, chop it finely with the brains and put the mixture in a pan. Pound pepper, ligusticum, and fennel seeds, moisten with liquamen and a little wine, and pour this into the pan over the brains and meat. When [the alica] has cooked enough, mix it with the sauce: dress the alica, a ladleful at a time, stirring, and melting it well so that it takes on the consistency of a thick soup.

APICIUS, *De re coquinaria* V.I.1

SEMOLINA WITH MEAT SAUCE (serves 6)

Salted water	4 cups	Fennel seeds	plenty
Semolina or spelt	9 oz	Nuoc-nam*	4-5 tablespoons
Olive oil	3 tablespoons	Wine	1 cup
Lamb brains	2	Ground meat	7 oz
Pepper	to taste		
*Ligusticum**	1 generous handful (or an equal amount of half celery and half parsley)		

Make a polenta with the water and the semolina or spelt. For the sauce, process in a blender the brains, previously boiled, cleaned well and trimmed, the celery and parsley (for the *ligusticum*), the pepper, the fennel seeds, the wine and the oil. Mix this sauce with the ground meat and cook slowly over very low heat. At this point you can either stir the sauce into the polenta and serve, or pack the polenta into a well-oiled ring mold, turn it out, and fill the center with the sauce.

POLENTA WITH OENOCOCTA SAUCE

A FILLING, TASTY ONE-DISH MEAL

Pour oenococta *sauce over the polenta. Use this sauce for chops, cooked semolina and* alica *and serve with pork chops, these too served with* oenococta *sauce.*

APICIUS, *De re coquinaria* V.I.2

POLENTA WITH WINE SAUCE (serves 6)

Salted water	4 cups	Celery	1 pinch
Semolina or broken spelt (farro)	9 oz	Garlic (to replace *laser*)	2 cloves
Pork chops	6	Red wine	1 generous cup
Pepper	to taste	Sweet Marsala	1 cup
Ligusticum*	3 1/2 oz	Pan juices from the chops	
Cumin	1 pinch	Water or broth	to dilute
Oregano	1 pinch	Salt	to taste

Cook the chops in a pan with a little oil, salt and pepper. Then add the semolina or spelt to the water to make a polenta. Process together in a blender all the herbs and spices, then dilute with the wine and the Marsala. Season with salt, and simmer the sauce slowly over a low flame. When it is almost done, taste for salt, bind with the starch and pour it over the polenta. Cook pork chops in the same wine sauce and serve the polenta on the side.

Minutal Marinum

AN EXCELLENT FISH SOUP

Throw the fish in a pot and add liquamen, *oil, wine and broth. Chop finely white leeks and coriander leaves; make small balls of fish and bone the other fish. Add sea nettles, well washed. When everything is cooked, pound* [in a mortar] *pepper,* ligusticum, *oregano, moisten with* liquamen *and cooking broth and pour everything into the pot. When it comes to a boil, break into pieces a* tracta *and bind [the soup], stir-ring. Sprinkle with pepper and serve.*

APICIUS, *De re coquinaria* IV.III.1

FISH SOUP (serves 6)

Fish and shellfish for soup, such as red mullet, grouper, scorpion fish, shrimp, mussels.

Salt	5 teaspoons or	Leeks	2
Pan juices	what there is	Nuoc-nam*	7 tablespoons
Ligusticum	1 handful	Pepper	to taste
Oregano	1 pinch	Olive oil	to taste
Broken pasta	7 oz		

Fillet, bone and cut up or slice the largest pieces of fish and set aside, reserving the heads and bones. To obtain the needed pan juices, brown very lightly in the oil the smaller fish with the reserved heads and bones of the large fish, then add first the wine, which should reduce to a few tablespoons, then the broth flavored with the leeks, sliced thin, 1 small handful of *ligusticum* leaves (or parsley and celery chopped together in equal quantities with additional pepper and oregano). Remove and reserve the usable flesh of the fish. Cook what is left over a low flame, then force through a sieve, discarding the heads, bones, etc., and put this thick soup in a pot over a lively flame. When the boil rises, toss into the pot the boned pieces of fish, sea nettles (very optional as they are impossible to find). At the end, add the broken pasta pieces and cook until tender.

Triangular Forum, portico

M*eat*

Ruins of the temple of Apollo

19

OFELLAE OSTIENSES
ONE OF THE BEST DISHES FOR DINNER

Cut the chop as far as the skin but without scoring it. Chop pepper, ligusticum, *dill, cumin, silphium, a laurel berry, moisten with* liquamen, *rub well and put everything in a baking pan with the* ofellae. *Let them marinate for two or three days. Then take them, thread them on to skewers [putting the loin back together] and put them in the oven. When they are done, separate the chops and make a sauce with pepper,* ligusticum, liquamen, *and sweet wine. Bring to a boil and then bind with starch. Pour the sauce over the chops and serve.*

APICIUS, *De re coquinaria* VII.IV.1

OSTIA CHOPS (serves 10-15)

Pork loin	4 1/2 lb	Dill*	1 pinch
Nuoc-nam*	12 tablespoons	Cumin	1 pinch
Pepper	generous amount	Garlic	4 cloves
*Ligusticum**	1 generous handful	Olive oil	small amount
Dry white wine	1 cup		

With a sharp knife, detach the meat almost completely from the bone. Open it like a book with the bones on one side and the layer of fat and meat on the other. Slice the loin into slices about 3/4 inch thick without, however, cutting the outer layer. Make a marinade with all the other ingredients. If you do not have the *ligusticum,* use an equal amount of half parsley and half celery. If you do not have the nuoc-nam, mix 1 cup water, 3 teaspoons salt and 3 anchovies dissolved over heat in 1/2 cup oil. Although it is not specified in the ancient recipe, it is advisable to add a little oil to the marinade and a cup of white wine: they will be needed to make the right quantity of liquid to pour over the piece of meat. Pour the marinade over the meat and put the pan in the refrigerator for a couple of days, turning the meat from time to time.

At the end, remove the meat from the liquid. Discard the liquid and re-form the loin on its bone attaching together the slices with long skewers stuck from one side to the other to hold it together during cooking. Put it in the oven for a couple of hours at 320°F (160°C) and keep an eye on it. When it is half done, throw a little white wine over it so it won't dry out. This will help to form a sauce with which you will continue to baste the roast until it is completely cooked and golden brown. Remove the roast from the pan; put the pan on the fire and deglaze with 1 cup Marsala or other sweet wine. Pour the pan juices into a saucepan and add:

Pepper	abundant
Ligusticum	1 generous handful
Broth	1 cup

Put the pan over a low flame and let the juices simmer slowly, then at the end bind with the starch and mix well in a blender. Taste for salt. If there is too much salt, dilute with water and bind with starch again to give the sauce the right consistency. A teaspoon of honey goes well in the sauce too. Put the sauce in a sauceboat and serve with the roast.

OFELLAE ALITER

SIMPLE, QUICK AND TASTY

Cook for a long time until well browned. Take one cyathus of best-quality liquamen, one cyathus of water, one cyathus of vinegar and one cyathus of oil. Put everything in an earthenware pan, fry and serve.

APICIUS, *De re coquinaria* VII.IV.4

PORK CHOPS (serves 6)

Pork chops	6 (about 2 lb)
Vinegar	4 tablespoons
Water	4 tablespoons
Oil	4 tablespoons
Nuoc-nam*	4 tablespoons

Place the chops in a pan just large enough to hold them and pour over them the nuoc-nam, vinegar, water and oil, which should just cover them. Cook over a lively flame until all the liquid is absorbed and the chops are nicely browned. If you don't have nuoc-nam, use 2 teaspoons salt dissolved in 4 tablespoons water and 2 anchovy fillets dissolved over low heat in oil, but the dish will suffer.

21

HAM

WONDERFUL FOR LARGE PARTIES

Take a ham and boil it with a great many dried figs and three bay leaves.
Skin it, cut a diamond pattern on it, and fill the incisions with honey. Then
make a pastry crust with flour and oil and cover the ham with it. When the
crust is cooked, remove from the oven.

APICIUS, *De re coquinaria* VII.IX.1

HAM EN CROÛTE (for a very large dinner)

Ham	6 1/2 lb
Flour	1 lb
Salt	1 tablespoon
Oil	10 1/2 tablespoons
Ice water	8 tablespoons

If you wish, you can follow the ancient recipe step by step. Naturally, you will need a large number of guests to dispose of an entire ham. On the other hand, you cannot cook pieces of ham, because they do not come out right. In Roman times, pre-cooked ham did not exist and therefore it was necessary to start with a raw one. But today, there is nothing to stop you from skipping the first step of this procedure and buying a precooked ham. For 40 persons you'll need a ham weighing about 6 1/2 pounds. First, skin the ham, then cut a diamond pattern holding the knife at an angle to the surface, then rub with honey. In the meantime, you will have quickly made a pate brisee using oil instead of butter.

Like all pates brisees, it must be handled quickly and not worked too much. Some people even mix the ingredients with a large blade to prevent contact with the heat of the hands. Using a rolling pin, roll out the dough on a sheet of plastic wrap. Put the ham on top of the pastry sheet and generously spoon on more honey. Wrap the ham carefully in the pastry, helping yourself with the plastic. Then place the ham delicately in an oiled roasting pan, making sure that the dough is sealed tightly and does not tear. Once you have removed the plastic, decorate the top with bits of pastry and brush with beaten egg yolk. Finally, put the pan in the oven at 320°F (160°C) until the crust is cooked and golden brown. The ham can be eaten either hot or cold, but cold is better.

Roast kid

A SIMPLE BUT GOOD RECIPE

Rub well with oil and pepper. Sprinkle it with pure salt with plenty of coriander seeds. Put it in the oven and serve it roasted.

APICIUS, *De re coquinaria* VIII.VI.8

ROAST KID (serves 6)

Kid (shoulder and leg)	3 lb 5 oz
Salt	3 teaspoons
Pepper	to taste
Coriander seeds	generous amount
Oil	1 1/2 teaspoons

This ancient recipe does not need much explanation in that it is more or less current today. In fact, it is so simple that it is unlikely that a similar recipe cannot be found in a modern cookbook. The only advice is this: I do not know whether most Romans actually loved coriander seeds as much as the compiler of *De re coquinaria* would have us believe, but I do know for certain that today not everybody likes the taste, so be careful how much you use. Otherwise, all you have to do is dry the kid well, rub it with oil, sprinkle it with salt and put it in the pan.

Put it in an oven preheated to 320°F (160°C) for an hour and a half, until it is cooked through and nicely browned. Baste every so often with its juices, and when it is almost done, splash it with white wine and a little vinegar.

23

ESICIA OMENTATA

TASTY WITH COCKTAILS TOO

Take ground meat with soft white bread crumbs soaked in wine. Pound to-gether pepper, liquamen *and, if you wish, seeded myrtle berries. Form little meatballs and insert pine nuts and peppercorns. Wrap them in the caul fat and brown them with* caroenum.

APICIUS, *De re coquinaria* II,I,7

MEATBALLS IN CAUL FAT (serves 6)

Ground meat	14 oz
Soft bread crumbs	2 oz
Red wine	1/2 cup
Pepper	1 generous pinch
Salt	1 teaspoon or 2 tablespoons nuoc-nam*
Seeded myrtle berries	to taste
Caul fat	amount needed for 18-20 meatballs
*Caroenum**	as needed

Soak the bread crumbs in the wine and knead with the ground meat and the myrtle berries, chopped. Form the mixture into balls and in the center of each insert peppercorns (if you like them) and pine nuts. Then wrap them in the caul fat and brown them in a pan with oil and a little Marsala.

24 PORK LIVERS

EXCELLENT EITHER FOR DINNER OR SNACKS

Cut the liver in pieces, moisten it in the liquamen, *chop pepper* ligusticum, *two laurel berries, wrap it in the caul fat, roast it on the grill and serve.*

APICIUS, *De re coquinaria* VII.III.2

PORK LIVERS WRAPPED IN CAUL FAT (serves 6)

Pork livers	1 lb Nuoc-nam* (for the marinade) 3 tablespoons or
Salt	1 teaspoon
Caul fat	7 oz
Ground pepper	to taste
*Ligusticum**	1 handful
Nuoc-nam* (for cooking)	1/4 cup

Soak the caul fat in cold water. Cut the liver into pieces. Make a marinade: process together in a blender all the herbs and spices (you can replace the *ligusticum* with an equal amount of half celery and half pars-ley), then dilute with the nuoc-nam (which you can replace with a scant teaspoon of salt and an anchovy fillet dissolved in oil). You can also substitute bay leaves for the laurel berry. Marinate the livers. After two hours, drain the livers of the marinade and the caul fat of the water, and wrap each piece of liver with a bay leaf in a little square of caul fat and close with a toothpick. They can be either grilled or browned in a heavy skillet with a little oil.

25 LIVER

LESS FATTY AND MORE WHOLESOME THAN THE USUAL LIVER PATES

Cook liver, mince it and add pepper or liquamen *or salt and add oil. Liver of hare, kid, lamb or chicken — and if you wish form it into a fish in a small mold. Pour green oil over it.*

APICIUS, *De re coquinaria* IX.XIII.1

LIVER PATE (serves 6)

Lamb liver	9 oz
Chicken livers	9 oz
Pepper	to taste
Onion	1
Nuoc-nam*	2 tablespoons or 1 teaspoon and 2 anchovy fillets
Oil	2 tablespoons
Bay leaves	2 or 3

Clean the livers well, saute the onion and add the nuoc-nam (or else dissolve a couple of anchovy fillets in olive oil over low heat). Add a couple of bay leaves for fragrance. Add the livers to the pan, season with pepper, and moisten with a little Marsala. Check whether the nuoc-nam or anchovies provided enough salt, and add a little more if needed. Now, process in a blender with just the little bit of liquid that will be left in the pan plus a little oil — just enough to make a mixture that is smooth but firm enough to mold. Pour the mixture into a mold lined with paper, chill, and when ready to serve, turn it out and decorate.

Patina cotidiana

VERY ELEGANT AND DELICATE

Crush boiled brains together with pepper, cumin and laser. *With* liquamen, caroenum*, *milk and egg cook them over a low flame in hot water.*

APICIUS, *De re coquinaria* IV.II.1

BRAIN FLAN (serves 6)

Brains	1 lb	Cumin	small amount
Nuoc-nam*	3 tablespoons or 2 teaspoons of salt	Garlic	1/2 clove
		Marsala	small amount
Onion and carrot	a few slices	Milk	2 cups
Ground pepper	to taste	Eggs	5

Soak the brains in cold water for 1 hour, then put them on the fire in cold, salted water with a few slices of onion and carrot. When the water comes to the boil, lower the flame and let simmer for about 20 minutes. As soon as the brains are done, put them back into cold water and, when they have cooled completely, skin and trim them. Force them through a sieve, or process in a blender, adding a mixture of ground pep-per, ground cumin and minced garlic diluted with Marsala. Beat the eggs lightly in the milk and add this to the brain mixture. Oil a smooth-sided mold and set it in a pan of water in an oven at preheated to 285°F (140°C) for 1 hour, until the mixture is quite firm. Test for doneness with a toothpick. Turn out on a serving plate, sprinkle with pepper, and serve.

LUMBI ET RENES (KIDNEYS)

DELICIOUS, ESPECIALLY FOR A BARBECUE

Split them in two and open them, sprinkle with ground pepper, pine nuts, minced (green) coriander. Then close them and sew them up, wrap them in the caul fat and brown in oil and liquamen. *At the end, roast either in the oven or on the grill.*

APICIUS, *De re coquinaria* VII.VIII

KIDNEYS (serves 6)

Pork or lamb kidneys	2 lb	Pine nuts	plenty
Nuoc-nam*	4-5 tablespoons or 2 teaspoons salt	Caul fat for wrapping	
Green coriander	1 handful		
Pepper	to taste		

Pork kidneys are preferable for this recipe. The kidneys must be very fresh and nice-looking with no dark coloration or greenish spots. Cut them on one side, leaving them attached on the opposite one, then put them in cold water with a little vinegar and let them soak in several changes of water until they have lost every trace of unpleasant odor. When they are ready, dry well and place them, open, on the work surface, sprinkle with pepper and cover with generous amounts of pine nuts and a goodly amount of minced green coriander (or since that is not always available, with parsley, which substitutes effectively). Sew them up so the stuffing does not fall out. At this point, roll them up in the caul fat (previously soaked in cold water) and brown in a skillet with a little oil and 3 tablespoons nuoc-nam (or 5-6 anchovy fillets dissolved in oil over low heat). They should be nicely browned outside. Then remove them from the skillet and finish cooking in a hot oven or on a grill), or, best of all, over coals. They should not be too well done. Remove the thread, slice immediately and serve hot.

PARTHIAN CHICKEN

A VERY TASTY DISH

Split the chicken and quarter it. Pound pepper, ligusticum, *a few caraway seeds, moisten with* liquamen *and flavor with wine. Put the chicken in an earthenware pot and put the condiment on the chicken. Dissolve some fresh* laser *in a little lukewarm water, put it on the chicken and cook. Sprinkle with pepper and serve.*

APICIUS, *De re coquinaria* VI.IX.2

Meat

PARTHIAN CHICKEN (serves 4)

1 chicken	3 lb 5 oz
Peppercorns	to taste
Ligusticum	1 handful
Caraway seeds	1 pinch
Nuoc-nam*	6 tablespoons or 3 teaspoons salt
Garlic (to replace *laser**)	2 cloves

Cut the chicken into pieces. Make the sauce in the blender with a little peppercorns, a handful of *ligusticum* (or the same amount of half parsley, half celery), a pinch of caraway seeds, everything diluted with the nuoc-nam (or 2 teaspoons salt dissolved in 3 or 4 tablespoons water and — since in this case it is almost certain that the *liquamen* of the recipe was *garum* — 4 anchovy fillets dissolved over heat in oil). Add to the blender jar also a couple of garlic cloves and stretch the mixture with lukewarm water so that it will be sufficiently liquid. Remember, however, that modern supermarket chickens are much more tender than ancient ones, which were proudly free-range. Therefore, if necessary, reduce the amount of water and perhaps add it only when you see that you need it. Cook over low heat until done. Serve with pepper.

CHICKEN *OXIZOMUM*

TASTY AND APPETIZING

A heaping acetabulum of oil, a little... [Here the text is missing but, since the recipe is practically identical to that of ofellae cotidianae, the missing ingredient should be water], *a scant acetabulum of* liquamen, *a somewhat scant acetabulum of vinegar; 6 scruples of pepper, 1 scruple of parsley and a bunch of leeks.*

APICIUS, *De re coquinaria,* IV.IX.3

CHICKEN IN PIQUANT SAUCE (serves 4)

1 chicken	3 lb 5 oz
Oil	6 tablespoons
Water	6 tablespoons
Nuoc-nam*	6 tablespoons
Vinegar	6 tablespoons
Pepper	1/4 oz
Minced parsley	1 good pinch
Chopped leeks	2

Cut the chicken into pieces. Mix the oil, the water, the vinegar and the nuoc-nam (or dissolve 2 teaspoons salt in 6 tablespoons water and add 4 anchovy fillets dissolved in oil). Season with the pepper, the parsley and the chopped leeks. If the liquid does not cover halfway up the chicken, add water. Put in a baking pan and cook until the chicken has absorbed all the liquid and is nicely browned.

CHICKEN *PAROPTUM*
A FLAVORFUL MAIN DISH

A small amount of laser, 6 scruples of pepper, 1 acetabulum of oil, 6 acetabula of liquamen, a little parsley.

APICIUS, *De re coquinaria* VI.IX.9

ROAST CHICKEN (serves 4)

1 chicken	3 lb 5 oz
Pepper	scant 1/4 oz
Minced parsley	1 tablespoon
Oil	6 soupspoons
Nuoc-nam*	6 tablespoons

Cut up the chicken and put it in a pan with the pepper, a little minced parsley, the oil, and the nuoc-nam (or 2 anchovy fillets dissolved in oil and 2 teaspoons salt dissolved in 6 tablespoons water). Cook the chick-en, turning it, until it is nicely browned.

Ham Wonderful for large parties

Ruins of the temple of Fortuna Augusta

THE ANCIENT RECIPES
OF MAGNA GRAECIA

The Nolan Gate seen from outside

The palaestra

AMIA

EXCELLENT ON THE BARBECUE OR FIREPLACE GRILL

"... As for the amia, cook it in autumn, when the Pleiades are setting, whatever fashion you like best. Why should I repeat for you word by word what you should do? You could not ruin it even if you wanted to. However, if you insist, dear Moschus, here is the best way to prepare this fish. Wrap it in fig leaves with a very little bit of marjoram. No cheese, no nonsense! Wrap it delicately in the fig leaves and tie them on top with a string. Then put them under the cinders and watch the time, so you don't burn it. Use the one from beautiful Byzantium if you want the best, but the ones caught near here are just as good. However, the farther you go from the Hellespont and travel on the glorious routes of the salty Aegean, it becomes not so good, and you will deny all my declarations."

ARCHESTRATUS OF GELA, in *Athenaeus*, VII.278 b-c

CHARCOAL-ROASTED FISH (serves 6)

1 roe tunny	4-4 1/2 lb
fig leaves	enough
salt	4 teaspoons
marjoram	2 pinches

Nothing to add: Archestratus says it all.

GONOS

AN UNFORGETTABLE DISH

Note: These are called "nunnata" in Sicily, "bianchetti" and "rossetti" in Genoa, and whitebait in English (in Sicily, which has preserved much from Magna Graecia, not least in marine terminology, the tiny newly hatched fish are still called "grommo", which means mucus).

"... Avoid all that mess of little fish just hatched except those of Athens — I mean the gonos, which the Ionians call `foam' — and accept them only when they have been caught in the sacred arms of the sea of Phalerum's beautiful bay. Those which are found off the sea-washed island of Rhodes are good if they are native. And if you want to taste them, you should buy them together with some nettles and sea anemones crowned with plumed tentacles. You must then mix them, and bake them in a pan after making a sauce of chopped herbs and oil..." A disciple of Archestratus adds that, given the small amount of heat needed to cook them, it is sufficient to put the whitebait in a hot pan and remove them as soon as they begin to sizzle.

ARCHESTRATUS OF GELA, in *Athenaeus* VII.285 c-d

HERBED SMALL FRY (serves 6)

Whitebait	2 lb 3 oz
Olive oil	the minimum needed for frying
Salt	to taste
Thyme	1 pinch
Marjoram	1 pinch
Oregano	1 pinch

Heat the oil, add the herbs, chopped, add the fish for a second. As soon as the fish begin to sizzle, drain immediately. Put everything on a serving plate, sprinkle with salt and serve piping hot.

FEMALE TUNA

The ancients did not have lemon before a certain period, but when they had it they used it mainly against moths or as an antidote to snakebites. Unfortunately, it never entered their heads that they might use it in cooking. "... *Use a tail-cut from a female tuna, a big female tuna, I repeat, whose mother city is Byzantium. Slice it and bake it to a turn, adding a little salt and oil. Eat the slices hot, dipping them in a piquant sauce. It is good also if you eat it plain, like the immortal gods in form and stature. But if you serve it sprinkled with vinegar it is perfection.*"

ARCHESTRATUS OF GELA, in *Athenaeus* VII.303 e-f

GRILLED TUNA STEAK (serves 6)

Fresh tuna	3 lb 5 oz
Salt	3 teaspoons
Olive oil	3 tablespoons
Vinegar	to taste

For this recipe, there is little to add to what Archestratus said.

KITHAROS

AN EXCELLENT RECIPE FOR TURBOT

"... As for the turbot, if it is white, firm and large, I ask you to boil it wrapped in leaves in clean salted water. But if it is reddish and not very large, bake it after piercing it well with a sharp knife. Flavor it at the last minute with plenty of cheese and oil. Because this fish likes people who enjoy to spend money and is prodigal."

ARCHESTRATUS OF GELA, in *Athenaeus* VII.306.b

TURBOT (serves 6)

If the turbot is large and white, boil it using this recipe:

Turbot	4 lb 6 oz	Salt	2 1/2 oz
Water	5 quarts	Vine leaves	several

Wrap the fish in the vine leaves and tie it. Put it in a pan of cold water and bring to the boil. Keep the water at a slow simmer, making sure it never boils violently. After 20 minutes check and, if done, drain and unwrap it.

If the turbot is not very large and has a reddish color, cook it in the oven or over coals.

2 turbots weighing about	2 lb each	Salt	4 teaspoons
Parmesan or pecorino cheese, grated	11 oz	Olive oil	plenty

Clean the fish. Just before cooking, salt it. Make a series of cuts on each side and fill these with the grated cheese and some oil. Rub the fish with more oil and put it in the oven in a well-oiled baking pan, or cook it over coals on a grill.

DOGFISH

A SIMPLE RECIPE

"... In the city of Torone buy slices of dogfish belly cut from the concave side. Sprinkle them with caraway seeds and a little salt and bake them. Do not add anything else, my friend, but yellow oil. But after it is cooked you can bring to the table the sauces and any condiment you wish to add. But if you stew it, never add the water from a sacred spring, nor wine or vinegar, but only oil, dried caraway seeds and a bunch of herbs. Cook it over coals, never letting the flame touch it, so as not to burn it. No! there are not many men who know how heavenly is this dish or who agree to taste it — these men are foolish as seagulls; it's as though they are paralyzed because, they say, that fish is a man-eater. But every fish eats human flesh if only it can..."

ARCHESTRATUS OF GELA, in *Athenaeus* VIL310, c-e

DOGFISH (serves 6)

Dogfish steaks	3 lb 5 oz	Olive oil	6 tablespoons
Salt	3 teaspoons	Caraway seeds*	a little

Rub the fish slices with plenty of oil, sprinkle with salt and caraway seeds. Place the slices on a grate over coals. The fish can be served with various sauces, one of which could be the excellent *salmoriglio* of Sicily, which among other things, has the advantage of being from Archestratus' home. It consists of oil, vinegar, oregano, a few whole cloves of garlic and a little water to help emulsify it when the sauce is beaten. Stewed dogfish is seasoned with caraway seeds, a little bunch of herbs and the same amounts of salt and oil, but never water. As for Archestratus' remark about the dogfish being a ferocious man-eater — don't let it bother you. The dogfish is a member of the shark family, but it is completely harmless and would never dream of going around biting people.

NUMB-FISH

A SIMPLE RECIPE FOR A FISH THAT CANNOT BE FOUND TODAY

"... a numb-fish browned in oil, wine, herbs and a little grated cheese".

ARCHESTRATUS OF GELA, in *Athenaeus* VII.314.d

NUMB-FISH EN CASSEROLE (serves 6)

Numb-fish	3 lb 5 oz
Salt	4 teaspoons
Dry white wine	1 cup
Herbs	1 small bunch to taste
Grated cheese	3 1/2 oz

Cook the fish slowly in an earthenware pan with the salt, the wine and the herbs. When done, add the grated cheese. Archestratus certainly did not have it, but the cheese that goes best is Parmesan. You be the judge. Cover the fish with the cheese and, as soon as it melts, remove the fish from the pan and put in on a platter.

SCARUS (SPARISOMA CRETENSE)

AN EXCELLENT RECIPE FOR DENTEX AND GILT-HEAD BREAM

"... In Chalcedon near the sea roast the good parrot-fish after washing it well. But you will find it good also in Byzantium, and as for its size, it will be as big as a round shield. Prepare it to cook it whole in the way that I will tell you: cover it with oil and cheese, hang it in a hot oven and roast it till just done. Sprinkle it with salt mixed with caraway seeds and yellow oil pouring the divine fountain from your hand..."

ARCHESTRATUS OF GELA, in *Athenaeus* VII.320 a

SCARUS (serves 5)

1 large scarus	3 1/2-4 lb
Salt	2-4 teaspoons
Oil	6 tablespoons
Cheese	11 oz
Caraway seeds*	7 oz

Scale, clean and wash the fish. Put it in a pan and cover it with oil and cheese (better to make crosswise incisions on both sides of the fish and rub well with salt, oil and cheese). Archestratus' oven is simply the old country oven that was placed on top of coals then covered with more coals. Today we have our wonderful modern ones, so put it in the oven at 320°F (160°C) for 45 minutes. When it is done, put it on a platter, sprinkle it with more salt and the caraway seeds, pour over it some top-quality extravirgin olive oil, and serve.

BREAM (*SARGOS*)

EXCELLENT

"... when Orion is setting in the heavens and the mother of the wine-bearing bunches begins to drop her tresses, then have yourself a roast sargos covered with cheese, big, hot and sprinkled with very sharp vinegar. Its flesh, in fact, is tough, so remember to cook all firm-fleshed fish this way. But the good fish that have a naturally fatty and tender flesh, cook them with just a little salt, and baste them with oil, be-cause these contain within themselves the prize of joy..."

ARCHESTRATUS OF GELA, in *Athenaeus* VII.321.c

BAKED BREAM (serves 6)

2 breams each weighing about	2 lb
Salt	4 teaspoons
Grated cheese	12 oz
Oil	plenty

Make deep crosswise incisions on the sides of the fish and rub with the salt, the oil and the cheese. Bake it in the oven and serve it sprinkled with good-quality vinegar. The bream has firm flesh. Fish with more tender flesh, such as sea bass or gray mullet, should be cooked only with salt and sprinkled from time to time during cooking with a little oil.

SQUID
AN INTERESTING RECIPE

Alexis, a comic playwright of the fourth century B.C., whom we know only through the excerpts from his work preserved in Athenaeus, gives a recipe for stuffed flying squid: As for squid, I chopped their tentacles, then mixed them with a little lard and sprinkled them with seasoning and stuffed them with finely chopped greens..."

ALEXIS, in *Athenaeus* VII.326.e

STUFFED SQUID (serves 6)

Squids	6
Salt	1 teaspoon salt for each pound of squid
Vegetables	as desired
Lard	3 1/2 oz
Olive oil	enough for cooking and dressing

Chop the tentacles and the lard and add some chopped greens, which have been either boiled or boiled then sauteed, then add some oil. Stuff the squids with the mixture and sew them up so that the stuffing does not come out during cooking. Now put the squid in an earthenware pan, add plenty of oil and a pinch of salt. Finally, put in an oven at 320°F (160°C) for 30 minutes.

GILT-HEAD BREAM (*CHRYSOPSOS*)
A REGAL DISH

> "... *Do not forget the fat gilt-head from Ephesus which some there call 'Ioniscus.' Buy this creature of the sacred Selinus. Wash it with care, then roast it and serve it whole even if it is ten cubits long...*"

ARCHESTRATUS OF GELA, in *Athenaeus* VII.328.b

Baked gilt-head bream (serves 6)

Gilt-head bream	3 lb 5 oz
Salt	3 teaspoons
Olive oil	7 tablespoons

The area around Ephesus is still famous for gilt-head bream, called *chippura* in Turkish. Rub with salt and oil and bake for 30 minutes at 320°F (160°C). In antiquity, the fish would have been sprinkled with vinegar, but today we use lemon

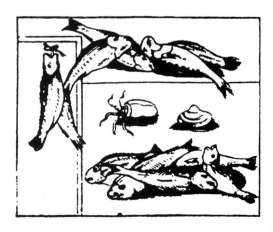

THE RECIPES OF THE LATE ROMAN EMPIRE

Courtyard of the gladiators' barracks

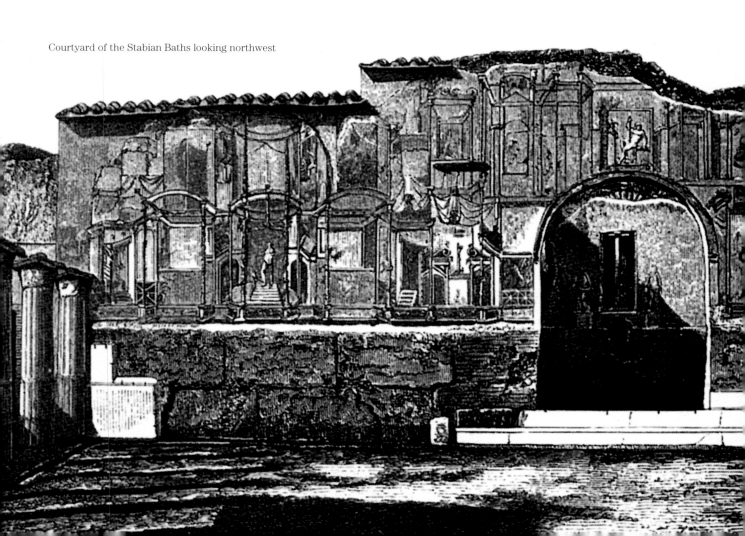

Courtyard of the Stabian Baths looking northwest

BAKED LOBSTER

Split the lobsters as usual leaving it in its shell, then moisten it with pipera-tum (pepper sauce) or coriandratum (coriander seed sauce) and roast it on the grill. As soon as it is dry, add on the same grill the liquid and let it dry up little by little, and continue until the lobster is completely cooked. Then serve.

APICIUS, *De re coquinaria* IX.I.2

GRILLED LOBSTER (serves 6)

6 lobsters	14 oz each, or 5 1/4 lb altogether
Pepper	plenty
Rue	a little
Marsala	1/2 cup
Dry white wine	1/2 cup
Salt	5 teaspoons in a little water
Anchovy fillets	2
Oil	3 tablespoons

If you have the nerve, split the live lobsters in two. If not, try another recipe. Unfortunately, these animals must be put on the fire still alive. Once you have done the deed, put the lobsters immediately on a grill over coals or on a preheated very hot heavy cast-iron skillet or, better, bar-becue. Moisten with the previously made pepper sauce. To make the sauce, process together in a blender the pepper, the rue, the sweet wine and the white wine, the salt and, even if the recipe does not say so — be-cause, as it was aimed at professional cooks, it omitted the most obvious things — the oil in which the anchovy fillets have been dissolved. During cooking brush the lobster continu-ously with the sauce so that the flesh will not dry up and become hard. Be careful not to overcook, because, when the lobster becomes tough, it loses all flavor.

HERB MARINADE FOR FRIED FISH

A TASTY COLD DISH THAT TASTES EVEN BETTER THE NEXT DAY

Fry the fish of your choice after washing it. Chop pepper, cumin, coriander seeds, laser *root, oregano, rue. Pulverize well, add vinegar, dates, honey, defrutum, oil,* liquamen. *Mix everything, pour it in the pot and bring to a boil. When it has boiled, pour it over the fried fish, sprinkle with pepper and serve.*

APICIUS, *De re coquinaria* X.I.1

MARINATED FISH (serves 6)

Small fish for frying	11 oz	Dates	flesh of 6
Pepper	plenty	Vinegar	12 tablespoons
Cumin	1 pinch	Oil	from frying the fish
Coriander seeds	1 pinch	Salt	1 pinch
Garlic	2 cloves	Anchovy fillets	2
Oregano	plenty	Honey or sugar	about 2 teaspoons
Rue (optional)	very little		

The fish should preferably include whitebait, anchovies, small red mullets, and other small fish. Marinated fried fish (called *scapece* in Naples) keeps for several days and is eaten cold. Wash and dry the fish, dredge it with flour, then fry in very hot oil and drain it on paper towels. Put the fried fish in an earthen-ware bowl. Pound the other ingredients in a mortar, or chop them in a blender. Put this mixture in the skillet, right in the oil in which the fish was fried, and cook slowly and thoroughly. Remove from the heat and immediately pour this marinade, still boiling hot, over the fish. Let cool, then refrigerate for one or two days before serving.

BAKED FISH
A GOOD AND ELEGANT RECIPE

*Take the fish, clean them and roast them but without cooking them completely;
then remove the flesh and prepare the oysters. Put in a mortar 6 scruples of
pepper, moisten with* liquamen *and pulverize. Then add 1 cyathus of* liquamen,
1 cyathus of wine, 3 ounces of oil and the oysters. Boil this oenogarum. *After
boiling, oil a baking pan, put in the flesh of the fish and pour over the oyster
sauce. Bring to a boil and as soon as it boils break 11 eggs and pour them
over the oysters. When they have cooked, sprinkle with pepper and serve.*

APICIUS, *De re coquinaria* IV.II.31

FISH PIE WITH OYSTER SAUCE (serves 6)

Oysters	12	Nuoc-nam*	6 tablespoons
(or mussels or clams)		Wine	6 tablespoons
Dentex, gilt-head bream	3 lb 5 oz	Oil	6 tablespoons
or gray mullet		Pepper	scant 1/4 oz
Eggs	11		

Scale, clean and wash the fish. Season it with salt and oil and put it in the oven until it is half cooked. Then take it out, and remove all the skin and bones. Make the sauce: mix the oysters, the pepper, the wine and the nuoc-nam (or a brine of 6 tablespoons water, 2 teaspoons salt and 3 anchovy fillets dissolved in boiling oil) and boil for about 15 minutes. In an oiled pan, put the cleaned fish and pour over it the oyster sauce. Put the pan on the fire until the fish is completely cooked. At this point, break the 11 eggs into a bowl, beat well as for an omelet and pour them into the pan with the fish. When it is cooked on one side, turn it over like a pancake and cook on the other. Remove from the fire, sprinkle with pepper, and serve.

FISH IN A PAN

A NEW WAY TO COMBINE FISH AND EGGS

Take fresh fish. Put it in a pan and add oil, liquamen, *wine, bundles of leeks and coriander. While it is cooking, chop pepper, oregano,* ligusticum *and the bundles which you have cooked. Reduce them to a mush and moisten with the sauce from the pan. Add to this raw eggs, work everything well, pour in the pan and let it bind. When everything is cooked, sprinkle with pepper and serve.*

APICIUS, *De re coquinaria* IV.II.27

FISH PIE (serves 6)

Fresh fish	3 lb 5 oz	*Ligusticum**	1 handful
Olive oil	6 tablespoons	Oregano	generous amount
Nuoc-nam*	6 tablespoons	Eggs	11
Dry white wine	6 tablespoons	Water	as needed
Pepper	generous amount		

Scale, clean and fillet the fish but only those of a certain size. For this recipe even very tiny fish, such as whitebait, work well. Put the fish in a pan just large enough to hold them and add the nuoc-nam (or 3 teaspoons of salt dissolved in water and 2 anchovies dissolved in oil), the wine and enough water almost to cover the fish. The fish should not be completely covered with liquid. While the fish cook, chop the pepper, the oregano, and the *ligusticum* (or a mixture of half celery, half parsley). Moisten the mixture with the liquid from the pan and add eggs (bear in mind that, if the quantity of sauce remaining in the pan is about 1 cup, you will need 11 eggs). Beat everything well and, when it is completely blended, pour in the pan and cook. As soon as the eggs have set and the pie is browned on both sides, slide it onto a serving plate, sprinkle with pepper and serve.

BAKED FISH

EXCELLENT RECIPE FOR FISH COOKED IN CLAY

Clean the fish carefully [removing the internal organs and all the scales]. *Then put in a mortar salt and coriander seeds; pound well. Coat the fish generously with the mixture and put it in a pan, cover it, and seal the lid with plaster. Then put it in the oven and cook. When the fish is done, remove from the pan, put it on a platter, sprinkle with strong vinegar and serve.*

APICIUS, *De re coquinaria* X.I.4

FISH COOKED IN A CLAY POT (serves 6)

1 large fish	3 lb 5 oz
Coarse salt	a lot
Coriander seeds	a lot
Vinegar	to taste

Clean and scale the fish and wash well, then put it in an earthenware baking pan that has its own lid. The pan should be just large enough to hold the fish. Pound together in a mortar a great deal of coarse salt and coriander seeds, keeping in mind that the fish must be completely buried in the mixture. Cover the fish with the mixture and seal the lid on as for chicken cooked in a clay pot. Put the fish in a preheated oven at 320°F (160°C) for 45 minutes. When the time is up, open the pan, scrape away all the salt and coriander and put the fish on a platter. Sprinkle the fish with vinegar, as in the ancient recipe. The Romans had lemons but considered them useful only against moths — like camphor.

NASIDIENUS' SAUCE FOR BOILED MORAY EEL

A TYPICAL SAUCE EMBELLISHED BY HORATIAN SATIRE

This sauce is make like this: first-press oil from Venafrum, garum made with the juice of Spanish fish, wine aged five years, but make sure it comes from this side of the sea when you have to cook it. If, however, you have to add it after cooking, Chian wine is better; white pepper and don't forget the vinegar made from the Methymnaean grapes. I am the first, declares Nasidienus, to add green rocket and bitter elecampane.

HORACE, *Satires* II.8.45-52

NASIDIENUS' SAUCE FOR BOILED MORAY EEL

Extravirgin olive oil
Anchovy fillets or tuna roe
Plenty of red wine
Good-quality vinegar
Chopped herbs

To substitute for Spanish *garum,* dissolve the anchovy fillets in the extravirgin olive oil, then add a generous handful of chopped herbs and dilute with red wine and vinegar. Then boil the sauce briefly.

CURTILLUS' SAUCE
ONE OF THE MOST DELICIOUS SAUCES I KNOW

Curtillus showed, however, the way to make the preceding sauce more fla-
vorful with sea-urchin eggs split it two and with their liquid which is better
than any brine.

HORACE, *Satires* II.8.45-52

SAUCE OF SEA-URCHIN EGGS (serves 6)

Sea urchins	50-70
Garlic cloves	3 or 4
Anchovy fillets	4
Extravirgin olive oil	as needed

This is still made in Sicily, where it is used for spaghetti. For 6 persons, you will need 50 to 70 sea urchins. Put plenty of oil in a skillet. Add the garlic cloves, cook, and remove them before they begin to brown. Dissolve the anchovy fillets in the oil, and at the end add the eggs of the sea urchins, previously well dissolved in a puree. Pour immediately over the spaghetti. This sauce is also wonderful over both boiled and baked fish.

INDIAN-STYLE PEAS

AN EXCELLENT RECIPE FOR SMALL CUTTLEFISH

Cook the peas. Skim off the froth, slice thinly some leek and green coriander and put them in the pot and bring to a boil. Then take some tiny cuttlefish and cook them in their ink. Add oil, liquamen, wine and a bundle of leek and green coriander. Cook. When done, pound pepper, ligusticum, oregano, a tiny bit of caraway and moisten with the cooking juices, wine and sweet wine. Slice the cuttlefish and throw them in with the peas. Sprinkle with pepper and serve.

APICIUS, *De re coquinaria* V.III.3

CUTTLEFISH IN ITS INK WITH PEAS (serves 6)

Small cuttlefish with their ink	2 lb 3 oz	Shelled fresh peas	1.1 lb
Leek	1	Oregano	1 good pinch
Caraway seeds*	1 pinch	Pepper	plenty
Green coriander	2 bunches (you can substitute parsley)		
*Ligusticum**	1 handful (you can substitute parsley and celery)		
Nuoc-nam*	6 tablespoons (or 3 teaspoons salt and 3 anchovy fillets)		
Dry white wine	1 cup		
Sweet wine	3 tablespoons		

Boil the peas in salted water with the leek, sliced thin, and the coriander or parsley. Then clean the cuttlefish, but leave the ink sac, and put them in a pan with a little oil. While they cook, add the oil and the nuoc-nam, the dry white wine and a bundle made from a small leek and a sprig of parsley tied together. When the cuttlefish are quite tender, chop together pepper, a little celery and parsley, oregano, a very few caraway seeds and moisten this mixture with the liquid from the pan. Put this sauce in the pan, put the pan back on the heat, stirring, and add a little sweet wine (or even a bit of sugar) to soften the flavor. When everything is thoroughly blended, cut up the cuttlefish and add them to the drained peas. Let the flavors blend over heat, then sprinkle with pepper and serve.

The Street of Tombs looking toward the city

*V*egetables

The apodyterium

BOILED SWISS CHARD
A WONDERFUL WAY TO ADD INTEREST TO BOILED GREENS

Boiled chard is good served with mustard, a little oil and vinegar.

APICIUS, *De re coquinaria* III.XI.2

BOILED CHARD (serves 6)

Swiss chard	about 2 lb
Dijon mustard	2 teaspoons
Vinegar	1 tablespoon
Oil	3 tablespoons

Since Swiss chard is a bit insipid, it needs to be dressed with something that makes up for that defect. Boil the greens in salted water, drain well, and press between clean hands to remove all the water. Then in a small bowl make a dressing with 2 teaspoons strong mustard, 1 tablespoon of vinegar and 3 tablespoons oil, and dress the chard while it is still hot. It will be even better if you let it rest for a bit to let the flavors blend.

50

SWISS CHARD

A GOOD SIDE DISH

Take chopped chard and dried leeks. Boil them together, then put in a baking pan. Chop pepper, cumin, moisten with liquamen *and add a bit of sweet wine to give it a sweet base. Bring to the boil and serve immediately.*

APICIUS, *De re coquinaria* III.II.1

CHARD WITH DRESSING-1 (serves 6)

Swiss chard	about 2 lb
Fresh leeks	2
Pepper	generous amount
Cumin	1 pinch
Nuoc-nam*	3 tablespoons
Sweet wine	1/2 cup

Use tender, young chard. Chop the greens fine and also cut up a couple of large leeks. Since preserved leeks are not used today, use fresh. Put the vegetables in a pan and pour over them a sauce made of the pepper, the cumin and the nuoc-nam (or, even better, 4 anchovy fillets chopped and diluted in 1/2 cup oil with 1 teaspoon salt dissolved in a little water). Finish with 1/2 cup sweet wine to correct the flavor. Cook until the water of the chard and the liquid of the sauce have been absorbed and then serve.

51

SWISS CHARD
A DIFFERENT VEGETABLE DISH

*Chop finely leek, green coriander, cumin, raisins and flour, and throw
everything over ribs of chard. Bind the sauce, then serve with* liquamen, *oil,
and vinegar.*

APICIUS, *De re coquinaria* III.XI.1

SWISS CHARD WITH DRESSING-2 (serves 6)

Swiss chard	2 lb 3 oz
Leek	1 large
Coriander leaves	1 handful
Cumin	1 pinch
Sultana raisins	1 fistful
Flour	1 tablespoon
Oil	3 tablespoons
Vinegar	1 tablespoon
Nuoc-nam*	3 tablespoons

Clean the Swiss chard and boil it briefly. Let its flavor blend over low heat with a mixture of the following ingredients chopped together very fine: leek, parsley (if you don't have coriander leaves), the pinch of cu-min, then the raisins (plumped in warm water) and a little flour to bind the sauce. Evidently the chard should be drained, but not very dry, then sauteed in a skillet with the mixture of chopped ingredients. When the flavors have blended and the flour (whose role is to bind the cooking water) is completely cooked, dress the greens with a vinaigrette of vinegar, oil and nuoc-nam (it is better to replace the nuoc-nam with 4 anchovy fillets dissolved in oil and 1 tablespoon table salt).

BULBI, FOR LOVE

FOR COUPLES, YOUNG AND NOT SO YOUNG

For those who seek the joys of Venus, boil bulbi *in water, then, as is done also at legal weddings, serve them with pine nuts or with the juice of rocket and pepper.*

APICIUS, *De re coquinaria* VII.XIV.3: from a recipe of Varro

SOMETHING SPICY

This recipe needs no annotation. *Bulbi** are the very bitter, onion-like *lampacioni* which require a particular treatment to be edible. Evidently our distant ancestors had great faith in their virtue, in that they served them to honeymoon couples; but, just in case, they also added the juice of the exciting rocket and a goodly amount of pepper. Try it: the power of suggestion and faith always work miracles.

CARROTS OR PARSNIPS

A TASTY SIDE DISH

They are served fried dressed with oenogarum, *or they can be dressed with salt, plain oil and vinegar.*

APICIUS, *De re coquinaria* III.XXI.1-2

Carrots or parsnips (serves 6)

Carrots or parsnips	2 lb 3 oz
Peppercorns	20
Ligusticum	1 handful
Nuoc-nam*	4 tablespoons
Honey	1 teaspoon or
Sugar	1/2 teaspoon
Red wine	1/2 cup
Oil	3 tablespoons
Starch	as needed to bind the sauce

Slice the carrots or parsnips thin and fry them in the oil. Drain on several thicknesses of paper towel. Meanwhile make the sauce. Process in a blender the peppercorns, 2 ribs of celery and a handful of parsley, then add the nuoc-nam (or anchovies and salt), the honey or sugar and a little red wine. Add a little oil and boil well in a small pot over low heat. When the sauce is completely cooked, bind it with the starch, leave it on the heat for another few minutes and, at the end, pour it over the carrots. You can also serve the carrots very simply with oil, vinegar and plain salt.

SAUCE FOR CARROTS OR PARSNIPS

VERY DIFFERENT BUT INTERESTING

Cumin sauce for oysters and shellfish: pepper, ligusticum, parsley, dried mint, citronella leaves, malobathron, somewhat more cumin, honey, vinegar and liquamen.

APICIUS, *De re coquinaria* I.xv.1

SAUCE FOR CARROTS OR PARSNIPS (serves 6)

Carrots or parsnips	2 lb 3 oz
Ligusticum	1 handful
Parsley	1 handful
Dried mint	1 pinch
Cinnamon	to sprinkle
Cumin	2 tablespoons
Honey	1 teaspoon
Vinegar	1 tablespoon
Nuoc-nam*	4 teaspoons

Boil and slice the carrots or parsnips. Cook them in the same cumin mixture that Apicius recommends for mollusks: chop together pepper, a lot of cumin and, if you don't have *ligusticum,* use an equal amount of half celery and half parsley. You'll have to forget the citronella, which not even herbalists can supply; malobathron, which may have been a special kind of cinnamon, is no easier to find. If you really want to, you can sprinkle the mixture with cinnamon. Then bind all the ingredients with the honey, vinegar and brine and, if here we take *liquamen* to mean *garum,* also add anchovy fillets dissolved in hot oil, which tastes better on cold dishes than nuoc-nam does.

LENTICULAM DE CASTANEIS

A GOOD ACCOMPANIMENT FOR MEAT OR POULTRY

Take a new earthenware pot and put in the carefully cleaned chestnuts. Add water and a bit of baking soda and cook. When they are cooked, put in a mortar cumin, coriander seeds, mint, rue, laser root and pennyroyal, and pound everything well, moistening with vinegar, honey and liquamen. Add more vinegar and pour over the cooked chestnuts. Taste, and if anything is needed, add it. When you put them in the boletar [serving bowl] pour green olive oil over them.

APICIUS, *De re coquinaria* V.II.2

PUREE OF CHESTNUTS (serves 6)

Chestnuts	1 lb 1 oz	Rue leaves	1 pinch
Pepper	1 pinch	Garlic	1 clove
Cumin	1 generous pinch	Nuoc-nam*	2 tablespoons
Coriander seeds	1 pinch	Honey	1 teaspoon
Mint	1 scant handful	Vinegar	1 tablespoon
Pennyroyal	1 scant handful	Green olive oil	3 tablespoons

Carefully shell and peel the chestnuts. Boil them in water with a pinch of baking soda in an earthenware pot. Drain when cooked. Meanwhile, put in a blender jar the pepper, the cumin, the coriander seeds, the mint, the rue, the garlic and the pennyroyal. Process all these herbs and spices with the teaspoon of honey, 1 tablespoon vinegar and (if you don't want to use nuoc-nam) 4 anchovy fillets dissolved in 1/2 cup oil. Put the mixture in the earthenware pot with the chestnuts, and let the flavors blend over low heat. When all the liquid has absorbed, put the chestnuts in a food processor and process until the mixture becomes a puree. Taste, and if something is missing, add it and run the processor again. At the end, put the chestnut puree in a deep serving dish and dress with 3 tablespoons of green olive oil.

56 *FABACIAE*

AN INTERESTING SPRINGTIME DISH

Serve the beans with ground mustard, honey, pine nuts, rue, cumin and vinegar.

APICIUS, *De re coquinaria* V.VI.3

FRESH FAVA BEAN SALAD (serves 6)

Fresh fava beans	6 1/2 lb
Colman's Mustard	3 teaspoons
Honey	1 teaspoon
Pine nuts	to taste
Rue	to taste
Cumin	2 teaspoons
Vinegar	to taste

Shell the fava beans and boil in salted water. Make the dressing: mix the mustard powder with the honey and dilute with the vinegar. If you don't want it to be too hot, reduce the amount of mustard. Mix the boiled fava beans with the fresh rue, chopped coarsely, and the pine nuts, then pour over the dressing. Put in a serving dish, sprinkle with the cumin and serve.

LARGE LEEKS
TO SHOW HOW APICIUS' SAUCES CAN OFTEN BE REVISED AND RUINED

Cook in water and oil with a handful of salt. Then serve them with oil, liquamen *and wine.*

APICIUS, *De re coquinaria* III.x.1

LEEKS IN VINAIGRETTE (serves 6)

Leeks	8
Coarse salt	1 handful
Oil	3 tablespoons
Nuoc-nam*	2 tablespoons
Wine	1 tablespoon

This is a typical recipe from Apicius' book, reproduced here to show how often his recipes are modifications of old traditional ones. We might call them two-layered recipes, the first being what the Romans usually ate ("cook them in water with a fistful of salt"), and the second ("then serve them with oil, *liquamen* and wine") is the addition, some centuries later, of a mediocre cook who presumptuously wrote under the name of the famous gastronome. In transcribing the old recipe, he did not even remember that the leeks are here boiled with a handful of salt: therefore not only are they already salted but, given the quality of salt prescribed, they are salted quite sufficiently. The addition of *liquamen* (which is very salty) would make them inedible. It is also interesting to note that wine in this recipe is used instead of vinegar in the vinaigrette. This does not speak very well for the wines of the period — there must have been little difference between cooking wines and vinegar.

Vegetables

Turnips and Rutabaga

TASTY

Squeeze boiled (vegetables), then chop a lot of cumin, a little rue and some laser; *dilute with honey and vinegar;* liquamen, defrutum *and a little oil. Boil the turnips in this sauce and then serve.*

APICIUS, *De re coquinaria* VII.XIII.1

TURNIPS AND COLESEED (serves 6)

Turnips	2 lb 3 oz
Cumin	1 tablespoon
Rue	small amount
Garlic	1 clove
Honey	2 teaspoons
Defrutum*	2 teaspoons
Oil	3 tablespoons
Vinegar	1 tablespoon
Nuoc-nam*	4 tablespoons

Slice the turnips and boil until half done, then drain and squeeze well. Then chop together a generous amount of cumin with a little rue and a clove of garlic (in place of *laser*). Mix everything with the honey and *defrutum,* which will provide a little sweetness (if you don't have *defrutum,* increase the quantity of honey or add 1 tablespoon sugar). Finish with oil, salt and vinegar and (if you don't want to use nuocnam) 1 1/2 teaspoons salt and 4 anchovy fillets dissolved over heat in oil. Boil the turnips in this sauce. Taste for seasoning, and serve.

GUSTUM (APPETIZER) *DE CUCURBITIS*

A WAY TO GIVE WINTER SQUASH MORE FLAVOR

Squeeze the water out of some cooked squashes and arrange them attractively in a pan. Put in a mortar pepper, cumin, a tiny bit of silphium, a little rue: dissolve with liquamen *and vinegar, add a little* defrutum *to give color, and pour this sauce into the pan. When the squash has come to the boil two or three times, remove it from the fire, sprinkle with pepper and serve.*

APICIUS, *De re coquinaria* III.IV.1

MARINATED SQUASH (serves 6)

Squash	2 lb 3 oz	Oil	3 tablespoons
Pepper	plenty	Nuoc-nam*	4 tablespoons
Cumin	1 generous pinch	Vinegar	1 tablespoon
Garlic	1 small clove	Concentrated grape must	1 tablespoon
Rue	1 pinch		

Boil the squash, squeeze well, slice it and put it in a baking pan in a single layer. Separately process in a blender the pepper, the cumin, the garlic clove and a few leaves of rue. If you want to replace the nuocnam, use 2 teaspoons salt and a few anchovy fillets dissolved over low heat in oil, then add vinegar and a little concentrated must to give color to the squash and a touch of sweetness to take the edge off the sauce. If you don't have concentrated must, use honey or sugar. The squash will be paler in color, but just as good. Pour the dressing over the squash and bring to the boil 2 or 3 times. Then remove the pan from the flame, sprinkle with pepper and serve. Serve either hot and cold.

Sweets, Desserts and Cheeses

The suburban villa seen from the garden

60

Moretum

<small>Always a great success. Serve with cocktails.</small>

Here is the translation of the little poem attributed to Virgil: "... *on the hearth of his hut... you can see only a round cheese hanging from an old wicker string and an old bunch of dill. Our hero therefore went to stock up on other delicacies. Next to his hut there was a little garden... that day, therefore, thinking about what to get, he went to the garden and first thing, digging lightly in the earth with his fingers pulled out four heads of garlic with their fibrous roots. Then he picked some slender stalks of celery, the cold rue and coriander trembling on thin stems. When he had picked these herbs, he sat happily in front of the fire and in a loud voice asked the slave woman for a mortar. He freed the garlic from its knotty wrapping; then he removed from it the skin, which his hand scorn-fully threw on the ground, sweeping it far from him: he kept only the cleaned cloves which he scalded in boiling water, putting them then in the hollow of the stone. Here he sprinkled them with salt and added the cheese hardened in salt, finally threw on top of these the other herbs already mentioned. He passed with his left hand his garment under his hairy crotch and with the right began to crush under the pestle the perfumed garlic, mashing to a pulp the other herbs as well, which thus mingled their juices. His hand stirred rapidly. Little by little, each herb lost its green and of so many colors made one only that was not green because the white part of the cheese rebuffed this color, but neither did it remain white, in that the milk on contact with the herbs lost its whiteness. Often a whiff of sharp, pungent odors struck the nostrils of the man and his future meal made him wrinkle his nose. Just as often his hand was forced to dry his teary eyes, while he angrily accused the innocent smoke. The work was going well: the pestle no longer leapt about as at first, but, heavier, was made to trace large circles. At this point, Similus began to pour in, drop by drop, Palladian olive oil and to sprinkle a bit of vinegar on top. Then he mixed again, and when it was completely amalgamated, removed it, again cleaned the mortar carefully with two fingers and finally formed the whole into a ball to thus give it both the form and the name of* moretum.

Pseudovirgil, *Moretum*

MORETUM (garlic-flavored cheese)

Pecorino cheese (or other hard cheese)	11 oz
Garlic cloves	4
Celery ribs	2
Green rue	small amount
Coriander leaves	1 small handful
Olive oil	2 tablespoons
Vinegar	1 tablespoon

It is advisable to reduce to 4 cloves the 4 heads of garlic indicated in the poem. In Similus' day garlic heads must have been much smaller and Roman peasants' palates much more resistant than ours. Parboil the garlic cloves in a small saucepan and put them in the container of a blender or food processor with the cheese, the celery ribs, trimmed, and a little rue. Since the cheese is already salty, it is better to taste before adding any more salt. Process until the mixture is smooth, adding a few drops of oil as necessary, and finish with a few drops of vinegar. Finally, taste for seasoning and adjust as necessary.

COLUMELLA'S FRESH HERBED CHEESE

INTERESTING: SERVES AS A BASE FOR BETTER CHEESES

"Put in a mortar savory, mint, rue, [fresh leaves of] coriander, celery, chives, or if you don't have them, a green onion, lettuce, rocket, green thyme or catnip and also green pennyroyal, fresh cheese and salted too. Crush all this well and when it is thoroughly mixed, add a little vinegar and pepper. Put the mixture in a small bowl and pour some oil over it."

COLUMELLA, *De re rustica* XII.LIX.1

HERBED CHEESE

Fresh cheese	7 oz	Rocket	1 large pinch
Pecorino or cheddar cheese	3 1/2 oz	Fresh thyme	1 large pinch
Savory	1 bunch	Calamint	1 large pinch
Rue	a little	Pennyroyal*	1 large pinch
Green coriander leaves	a few	Mint	1 large pinch
Celery	1 rib	Oil	as needed
Scallions	2	Vinegar	to taste
Lettuce	1 leaf		

Put the cheeses in a mortar or blender with a sprig of savory, a very little rue and an equal amount of green coriander (or parsley) and a rib of celery, carefully trimmed, and the scallions. You can add the lettuce leaf too, but it is just for coloring. Finally, add the rocket, the fresh thyme or calamint, a little pennyroyal, and, finally, a handful of mint. Mint is characteristic of all Roman peasant dishes — they put it on everything. You can add more or less mint to taste, but there must always be some. Pound or process well to amalgamate the ingredients completely, adding extravirgin olive oil drop by drop. Finish with a little vinegar and ground pepper.

CHEESE WITH WALNUTS

DELICIOUS IF SOFT

Crush all the herbs listed above with large shelled walnuts, as many as you consider enough. Mix well, flavor with a little vinegar and pepper and cover with oil.

COLUMELLA, *De re rustica* XII.LIX.2

CHEESE WITH WALNUTS

Herb-flavored cheese	6 oz
Walnut meats	2 oz

Make the preceding recipe. Add the walnut meats and pound in a mortar or process in a blender. Check that the mixture does not get too hard and dry: the nuts tend to absorb oil, but the cheese must remain soft and creamy. The solution to this problem is gradually to add a small quantity of oil to give the mixture the consistency of cottage cheese. Finally, season with salt and pepper, taste, correct the seasoning with salt or, if needed, vinegar. The mixture will keep well in the refrigerator covered with a thin film of oil.

CHEESE WITH SESAME SEEDS

(In addition to) the green herbs listed above (add) also lightly toasted sesame. Flavor with vinegar and pepper and cover with oil.

COLUMELLA, DE RE RUSTICA XII.LIX.3

SESAME-FLAVORED CHEESE

Herb cheese . . . . 6 oz
Lightly toasted sesame seeds . . . . 1 oz

Toast the sesame seeds lightly in a skillet with a little oil, then add them to the basic herb cheese recipe (no. 61, above). Pound the mixture in a mortar or process in a blender. You can add oil gradually until the cheese reaches the right soft, light consistency. Add salt and pepper, taste and correct the seasoning. Then put the cheese in a small bowl, cover it with more oil and sprinkle with more toasted sesame seeds. Serve surrounded with toast on which to spread the cheese. The cheese keeps well in the refrigerator covered with a thin film of oil.

CHEESE WITH PINE NUTS

ONE OF THE BEST

Cut Gallic cheese or any other type you like in tiny pieces and pound it with pine nuts, if you have a lot; if not, with toasted hazelnuts from which the skin has been removed or with almonds, and mix them in the same quantity over the herbs used, then add a little peppered vinegar and pour oil over it. If you do not have the fresh herbs, you can also use dry.

COLUMELLA, *De re rustica* XII.LIX.4

CHEESE WITH PINE NUTS

Parmesan cheese	11 oz		Pine nuts	2 oz
Pennyroyal*	to taste		Oil	as needed
Thyme	to taste		Vinegar	to taste
Oregano	to taste		Pepper	to taste

"Gallic cheese" must have been a relative of Parmesan, in that Pliny speaks of a cheese of Luni, a town on the border between Tuscany and Liguria, whose round form weighed nearly 800 pounds. Even though it was not made in Aemilia, it seems to have been very similar to the large wheels of the Parmesan we know today. Columella notes that other hard cheese could be used.

Cut the cheese into pieces and put it in a mortar, or better a blender, with pennyroyal, thyme, oregano and savory (dried herbs may be used if fresh are not available) and the pine nuts. Amalgamate well, and if the mixture is too hard, add oil until the consistency becomes soft and creamy enough to spread on bread. Finally, flavor with vinegar and pepper. Taste, correct the

seasoning and put it in a small bowl. Pour a thin layer of oil on top, decorate with pine nuts and surround the container with pieces of toast on which to spread the cheese. If pine nuts are unavailable — or if you wish to vary the recipe — you can use toasted, peeled peanuts or peeled almonds. It keeps for a long time in the refrigerator if covered with a layer of oil.

Globi

THE SWEET ONES ARE WONDERFUL WITH COFFEE, THE SAVORY ONES WITH COCKTAILS

Make globi *like this. Mix fresh cheese with* alica *in the same proportions and the same way as for* libum *dough, using enough to make the desired number of* globi. *You will decide how much you will want to make. Put lard into a very hot bronze skillet and fry the* globi *one or two at a time, turning often with the help of two sticks. When they are done, remove them, drizzle them with honey, then sprinkle with poppy seeds and serve.*

CATO THE CENSOR, *De agricultura* LXXIX

GLOBI (serves 6)

Ricotta or any fresh cheese   8 oz
Salt. . . . . very little
Hard-wheat semolina . . . . 2 oz
Honey or sugar
Egg. 1
Oil for frying

Today *alica* is no longer made, but it is clear that it can be replaced with a good hard-wheat semolina or a very, very fine spelt. Knead the fresh cheese with the semolina, the egg and a pinch of salt. (Try to find a nonpasteurized fresh cheese as the pasteurized ones don't work as yeast.) Then, if you do not have an electric fryer, which is ideal for these sweets, use a small, rather tall heavy pot (the *globi* must be completely immersed in the fat). Cato mentions lard, which is superlative for frying, but nowadays it's better to use oil. With the help of a teaspoon, drop a little dough into the boiling oil. You can cook two or three at a time at most, keeping in mind that they expand as they fry. Then dip them in honey and sprinkle generously with poppy seeds in order almost to make a crust. This is a tedious job and I advise you to eat the *globi* simply rolled in sugar, or serve them as savory appetizers with just a sprinkling of salt and pepper.

PLACENTA

INTERESTING AS A CURIOSITY — TODAY WE CAN DO BETTER

"Take two pounds of wheat flour to make the outer crust, plus four pounds of flour and two of alica to make the tractae. *Soak the alica in the water and when it has increased in volume, put it in a clean kneading trough after having drained and dried it, then begin to knead. When it is well amalgamated, add a little at a time the four pounds of flour. Next, roll out this dough and form the* tractae, *then put them in a basket to dry. When they are dry, put them in a row, clean them with a cloth and spread them with oil. Cook them under* a testum [actually a large earthenware pot similar to our country ovens or so-called "bell" ovens] *with a very high flame. Now take the two pounds of flour, knead it with water and then make it into a very thin sheet. Take 14 pounds of very fresh sheep-milk cheese, put it in water and soak well in three complete changes of water. Then drain it, squeeze it, put it in a mortar, pound it, force it through a sieve and finally mix 4 pounds of honey. Now take a clean tile measuring 12 by 12 inches and cover it with oiled bay leaves. Over this spread* [making it hang down on the sides] *the sheet of flour that you prepared and begin to make the placenta. Put* a tracta *on the sheet; cover it with the cream, then put on top another* tracta *and cover it with cream and continue until all the* tractae *and all the cream are used up, finishing with* a tracta. *Now collect all the sweet in the sheet of pasta and close it on top. Put the placenta to cook on the hearth under* a testum *around which you will pile up the coals and that you will cover with these. It must cook long and slowly and you will uncover it every so often to see how it is doing. When it is done, moisten it with plenty of honey. This is the half-peck placenta."*

CATO, *De agricultura* LXXVI

PLACENTA (serves 12)

Flour	9 oz
Water	enough for kneading the dough
Salt	1 pinch Sheets of pastry cooked in the oven 5
Ricotta or any fresh cheese	11 oz
Honey	9 oz

Make a thin sheet of pastry with the flour and water. Beat the ricotta until smooth and mix it with the honey. Cover an oven tile with oiled bay leaves, spread the pastry sheet over it, letting the edges hang over the sides. Then put one of the sheets on top of it in the middle. (If you want to make them from scratch it is first necessary to knead water and hard-wheat semolina, then divide the mixture into five parts and roll them out like lasagne, then dry them, and when they are dry, brush them with oil and bake them briefly. It is a great deal simpler to use matzos or any equivalent.) Whatever type you use, cover it with a layer of the cheese cream and continue alternating sheets and filling until all the ingredients are used up. Finally, pull up the outer sheet and close it in the middle. Oil the sweet and put it in at oven at 320°F (160°C) for at least 30 minutes. When it is golden brown, remove it from the oven, and pour over it plenty of honey.

DATES

DELICIOUS!

Pit the dates and stuff them with walnuts, or even pine nuts, or ground pepper. Roll them in salt and fry them with cooked honey, then serve.

APICIUS, *De re coquinaria* VII.XIII.1

STUFFED DATES (serves 10)

Dried dates	1 box
Walnut meats	30
Salt	just enough
Honey	plenty

Take a box of good-quality dates (they should not be sticky, and the skin should not come off easily). Pit them by making a cut on one side. Fill the cavity with walnut meats, pine nuts or even ground black pepper. The ones stuffed with walnuts are the best, but the others are not bad at all. Roll them in <salt and fry them in honey in a skillet until they are caramelized. It is difficult to understand the function of the salt in this recipe but, whatever it is, it works to perfection and the dates get caramelized much better than they would without it. As soon as the dates are fried, put them on an oiled plate, as for caramelized fruit, to prevent sticking. While they are still piping hot, insert toothpicks to make them easier to eat.

PULTES TRACTOGALATAE

A WHOLESOME AND PLEASING SWEET

Put a pint of milk and a little water in a new saucepan and bring to the boil over a slow flame. Break into pieces three round, quite dry, sheets of tractae, *and throw them in the milk. Stir constantly so that the porridge will not stick to the bottom of the pan. When it is cooked well and while it is still on the fire, add the honey.*

APICIUS, *De re coquinaria* V.I.3

MILK PUDDING (serves 4)

Milk	2 cups
Water	a little
Small pasta for broth or rice	3 1/2 oz
Honey	to taste

This sweet is the ancestor of the Italian *riso al latte*. Rice could even be used in this recipe, but as Apicius speaks of *tracta,* it is better to use the small pasta made to be used in broth. Cook the pasta or rice in the milk mixed with a little water. When it is cooked, add honey until the pudding is sweet enough.

DULCIA
A HOMELY AND APPETIZING SWEET

Break white bread from which the crust has been scraped off and break it into pieces larger than a mouthful. Soak them in milk and fry them in oil, cover them with honey and serve.

APICIUS, De re coquinaria VII.XIII.2

HONEY BREAD (serves 6)

Day-old bread	12 slices
Milk	1 cup
Oil	for frying
Honey	12 tablespoons

Cut a loaf of day-old bread into slices about 3/4 inch thick. Remove the crusts and dip the slices into a bowl of milk. Fry them in very hot oil, drain well on paper towels, put them on a plate and pour honey over them. This dish is still made today to use up stale bread and make a wholesome sweet for children. The only difference is that today we sprinkle the bread with sugar.

PEPPERED SWEETS

AN EXCELLENT PUDDING

Chop pepper, pine nuts, honey, rue, sweet wine and cook with milk and tractae. *Cook this cream with a little egg. Serve drenched in honey and sprinkled with pepper.*

APICIUS, *De re coquinaria* VII.XIII.4

PEPPER CUSTARD (serves 6)

Milk	4 cups
Rice or tiny pasta	7 oz
Pepper	plenty
Pine nuts	1 handful
Rue	a few leaves
Egg yolks	3
Honey	
Wine	1/2 cup

Mince pepper, pine nuts and a very little rue, and amalgamate everything very well, adding the honey and a little wine. Then add to this condiment the 4 cups of milk and cook in it the rice or pastina. Substituting *tractae* broken up into tiny pieces for the rice does not change the flavor or the consistency of the sweet in that the purpose of the *tractae is* only to bind and solidify the cream, leaving it somewhat grainy. At the end, add the 3 egg yolks and stir until the mixture is creamy, but do not let the eggs scramble. When the sweet is done, put it in a serving bowl, cover it with honey, and sprinkle with lots of pepper.

SEMOLINA SWEETS

AN EXCELLENT HOMELY DESSERT

Take some semolina and cook it in very hot water until it becomes a very hard porridge. Then spread it in a skillet. When it has cooled, cut it as for sweets and fry these pieces in best-quality oil. Drain them, moisten them with honey, sprinkle with pepper and serve. The sweets come out better if instead of water you use milk.

APICIUS, *De re coquinaria* VII.XIII.6

SEMOLINI (serves 6)

Semolina	9 oz
Milk	4 cups
Salt	1 pinch
Oil	for frying
Pepper	plenty
Honey	plenty

This too is a traditional sweet that used to be made in Italian homes. Cook the semolina in 4 cups of milk with just a pinch of salt. When the mixture is dense, spread it on a tray and, as soon as it is cool, cut it in squares and fry these in oil. Drain well on paper towels and then drench them in honey and sprinkle with pepper. In modern times, instead of honey, they are sprinkled with sugar, and the pepper is omitted, which is too bad as it goes very well.

72

Tiropatina
THE ANCESTOR OF CREME CARAMEL

Take as much milk as you think you need for the pan you have chosen. Sweeten the milk with honey, as for milk sweets, and add 5 eggs for every hemina of milk. Dissolve everything well so it is well amalgamated and strain it through a sieve into an earthenware pot. Then cook over a slow flame; when it has set, sprinkle with pepper and serve.

APICIUS, *De re coquinaria* VII.XIII.7

FLAN OR CUSTARD (serves 6)

Milk	4 cups
Honey	plenty
Eggs	10
Pepper	to taste

For a ring mold, 12 inches in diameter and 4 inches high, take 4 cups of milk and dissolve the honey in it, tasting for sweetness (it should be very sweet because afterwards the eggs will be added). Mix well with the milk the 10 eggs, beaten as for an omelet, and pour the mixture through a sieve into the mold. Cook for an hour in a very low oven, preferably set in a pan of boiling water. Then unmold the sweet and sprinkle with plenty of pepper — it's really very good.

MILK OMELET

A VARIATION ON *OMELETTE SUCRE*

Four eggs, half a liter of milk, 1 ounce of oil, mixed well. Put a little oil in a thin skillet, heat it, then add the mixture. When it is cooked on one side, turn it, then put in on a serving plate, drench with honey, sprinkle with pepper and serve.

APICIUS, *De re coquinaria* VII.XIII.8

MILK OMELET (serves 4)

Eggs	4
Milk	2 cups
Oil	1 tablespoon
Honey	plenty
Pepper	plenty

Mix the eggs, the milk and the tablespoon of oil. Heat a little oil in an omelet pan, then pour on the milk and egg mixture. Let it thicken and, when it has reached the necessary consistency, turn it over and cook on the other side. Slip it onto a serving plate, drench it with honey and sprinkle with pepper.

CASSATA OF OPLONTIS

(Serves 15-20.) No recipe exists for such a sweet; it has been reconstructed on the basis of a wall painting found in one of the *triclinia* of the Roman villa of Oplontis; but it is based on the principles of ancient pastry making and on its similarity to the traditional Sicilian dessert known as *cassata siciliana*.

Ricotta	3 lb 5 oz		Honey	1 lb
Dried apricots	12 oz		Prunes	12 oz
Sultana raisins	3 1/2 oz		Walnut meats	3 1/2 oz
Dates	10		Almond flour	12 oz
Powdered red pastry coloring				

These are the quantities for a baking pan 12 inches in diameter and 2 inches high. First of all, dice finely the dried fruits. Set aside the most beautiful fruits and all the dates for the decoration. Cook the walnuts and the pine nuts in the honey until they are caramelized into a brittle, then break the brittle into pieces. Force the ricotta through a sieve. Reserve about 3 ounces of it for the decoration of the top, which has to be snow white, and mix the rest with the honey, a little at a time. The ricotta should be very sweet, more or less as sweet as *a cassata si-ciliana* — which is very sweet indeed. The cream should be worked well because is must be extremely smooth, soft and light. At this point add the diced dried fruit and the pieces of nut brittle. Knead the almond flour with the honey and the red food coloring to make a bright red marzipan. Then line a baking pan with oven paper oiled on the inner surface so that it will come off easily when the *cassata* is turned out of the mold, leaving a smooth surface. Roll out the marzipan with a rolling pin to make a strip with which to line the sides of the mold and push it hard against the oiled paper. Fill the cavity with the ricotta cream and refrigerate in the coldest part of the refrigerator (but not the freezer) to set for at least a day. Turn the *cassata* out onto a round serving plate, delicately remove the oiled paper both from the strip of marzipan and from the top, cover the top with a thin layer of ricotta, which you should force through a sieve and work a little so that it is very smooth as well as white. Finally, decorate the sweet with the reserved fruit, imitating as far as possible the sweet in the Oplontis painting.

ROMAN AND MODERN MEASUREMENTS

Latin	Metric	U.S.-British
1 acetabulum	0.068 liter	6 teaspoons = 2 tablespoons
1 calyx	wine glass	1/2 cup = 8 tablespoons
1 cyathus	0.0456 liter	4 teaspoons
1 coclear	0.0114 liter	1 teaspoon
1 drachma	1/100 pound = 3/4 teaspoon	
1 hemina	1 cup	
1 libbra	3/4 pound	
1 quartarius	1/2 cup	
scripulum (scrupulus)	scant 1/4 teaspoon	
semuncia	2 heaping teaspoons	
sextarius	2 cups = 1 pint	
uncia	27.27 grams	4 1/2 teaspoons

1 teaspoon = 6 grams
1/2 teaspoon = 3 grams
1/4 teaspoon = 1.5 grams
1 tablespoon = 2 teaspoons = 18 grams
4 liquid teaspoons = 1/2 deciliter
3 tablespoons = 1 jigger
20 liquid tablespoons = 1 cup = 1/4 liter

Printed in Rome, August 2010
«L'ERMA» di BRETSCHNEIDER
by Tipograf S.r.l.
Via Costantino Morin 26/A